THE ☆ SECOND
AMERICAN
REVOLUTION

Also by James Patterson and Peter Kim

The Day America Told the Truth

THE ☆ SECOND AMERICAN REVOLUTION

★

JAMES PATTERSON
AND
PETER KIM

★

WILLIAM MORROW AND COMPANY, INC.

New York

It is the policy of William Morrow and Company, Inc., and its imprints and affiliates, recognizing the importance of preserving what has been written, to print the books we publish on acid-free paper, and we exert our best efforts to that end.

Library of Congress Cataloging-in-Publication Data
Patterson, James, 1947–
        The second American revolution / by James Patterson & Peter Kim.
        p.   cm.
        ISBN 0-688-11730-9
        1. Public opinion—United States.   2. United States—Social conditions—Public
    opinion.   3. United States—Politics and government—1993- —Public opinion.   I. Kim,
    Peter.   II. Title.
        HN90.P8P38   1994
        306'.0973—dc20   93-48960
                                                                                        CIP

Printed in the United States of America

First Edition

1 2 3 4 5 6 7 8 9 10

BOOK DESIGN BY MICHAEL MENDELSOHN/MM DESIGN 2000, INC.

DEDICATION

For Joon Hee Kim-Lo
and her courageous husband, Dr. YunYan Andrew Lo.

For Dr. Ronald Drusin, too, with deep gratitude;
and the heart transplant team at the Columbia
Presbyterian Medical Center who keep Joon Hee well.

ACKNOWLEDGMENTS

The authors wish to express their huge appreciation to Thomas Fields-Meyer, whose efforts, and wisdom, helped us take a mountain of information and statistics and turn it into a compelling story. This project couldn't have been completed without Tom's dedication and enthusiasm.

We are also indebted to Gilbert Tweed Associates, Inc., for the executive search of all executive searches. Gilbert Tweed provided not just intelligence, but heart. Lynn Bignell worked as though this was the most important executive search of her life, and perhaps it was.

CONTENTS

INTRODUCTION
THE PEOPLE'S AGENDA

Americans are ready to fix America.

The crises are mounting. Never before have so many problems of such magnitude piled up so unceasingly: Soaring crime rates. Floundering schools. A leadership vacuum.

Yet we're not giving up. We want to *do* something. Now.

We've grown tired of empty rhetoric, of broken promises, of debate without results.

We're tired of waiting. We're ready to take action.

This book is about moving from frustration to resolve. It's about acknowledging the challenges that plague the nation—and then finding solutions.

The Second American Revolution isn't conservative or liberal. It's not the brainstorm of any one individual or an interest group. It's not about lecturing or predicting the future.

It's about listening.

We started with questions. We interviewed hundreds of Americans about their concerns, their anxieties, their fears, and their hopes for America. We asked them to consider the problems perplexing the nation. And we went back—and asked thousands of them to find solutions, to set the course for the future.

To read the papers, to watch the nightly news, you'd think that Americans had given up on their country. You'd think citizens had lost faith in their government.

But we came up with ways to gauge the will of the people, and harness their power and resolve for the good of the nation. We found ways to take the politicians and bureaucrats out of the process, to let Americans solve their own problems.

We didn't find cynicism. We didn't find hopelessness. We found a determination to find creative solutions.

Americans are ready to fix America.

THE CRISES

To consider America in the 1990s is to face up to a catalog of crises:

- A government lacking genuine leaders.
- A democracy crippled by morally divisive issues.
- A mind-boggling national deficit.
- Cities torn apart by violence.
- Schools failing to educate our children.

To be sure, every era has its share of difficult issues. But as we near the twenty-first century, Americans are questioning the very ability of our system to confront the difficulties plaguing us.

Americans want to believe in America again.

We've become a nation divided—divided by ethnic strife, by political extremism, by fear and diminishing hope. Our leaders, meanwhile, test the waters with opinion polls and media coverage. But they don't spend enough energy listening to the people.

Our conviction is this: the solutions to the problems crippling America lie with the people who make up America. The problem: we've grown so large, and our institutions so bureaucratic, that it's become difficult for our leaders to hear the voices of the people.

Until now.

This book will change America—not by dictating, but by listening. Not by debating, but by forging consensus. Not by re-collecting the plans of our leaders—but by collecting the will of the people.

We've developed scientific, cutting-edge methods for bringing democracy into the twenty-first century, using the building blocks of democracy.

A first. Elections come and go. But never before has America seen a national referendum that so accurately measures the nation's concerns and so effectively collects the people's ideas for solving its pressing crises.

The issues. First we've asked Americans to identify which issues cause them the most concern.

The ideas. Then we've explored those problems, investigating their root causes, their impact, and what might be done to solve them. On every issue, we've consulted with experts and investigated how various approaches have succeeded—or failed—elsewhere.

The solutions. Finally, we've asked ordinary Americans—more than six thousand in all—for their advice. We haven't sought quick, shallow reactions. We've asked Americans to analyze the issues in their full complexity, and then to react. They've told us what their priorities are, and why, and how they want to tackle the problems.

VOICES, NOT NUMBERS

Our revolution isn't about polling statistics; it's about voices.

"Some people see things that are and say why?" said Robert F. Kennedy (borrowing from George Bernard Shaw). "I dream of things that never were, and say why not?"

This book won't compile opinions about our nation's failures. It will propose creative solutions—to set the stage for future successes.

The Second American Revolution will finally produce a blueprint for facing up to our nation's greatest challenges, for restoring Americans' confidence in their nation.

But it starts with listening.

Our process was unlike any election or referendum ever conducted. To ensure that our findings would be flawless, meaningful, and authoritative, we developed a strategy for a referendum that would be more accurate and representative than any election ever held. The ideas we collected didn't come through middlemen. They came from the people themselves.

THE METHOD: THE PEOPLE'S PROBLEMS, THE PEOPLE'S SOLUTIONS

Our goal was to give the power directly to the people—not the politicians, not the bureaucrats, not the media—to make the decisions. We wanted the people to:

A. Frame the issues

B. Devise the solutions

With that objective, we started with the two building blocks of democracy:

A. The town hall

B. The referendum

A SCIENTIFIC APPROACH

Our nation has grown too big and unwieldy to call an actual town-hall meeting. But we created a way for Americans to shift from passive *observers* of the process to active, creative *participants*—agenda setters, problem solvers. We employed advanced sampling and research-design techniques to listen to the people directly. Our method—straightforward, credible, and effective—had five phases:

- The local town hall
- The national town hall
- The quest for solutions
- The executive search
- The national referendum

THE LOCAL TOWN HALL

The essence of democracy is the town-hall meeting, where citizens can gather in one room and discuss—face-to-face—the issues that concern them. With all of our advanced research methodology, nothing could replace the genuine emotions, dynamics, and creativity of the town hall. To kick off our effort, we went to New England—where the American town hall was born—and assembled a sampling of Americans in a small town. The result was an inspiring lesson about Americans' concern, insight, and ingenuity in approaching their problems.

THE NATIONAL TOWN HALL

To gain a wider perspective, we took the idea of a town hall to a wider forum. We used the techniques of sampling methodology to gauge the pulse of America. We designed a questionnaire to provoke Americans to raise issues and concerns—just as our local town hall provided a forum for open and honest discussion.

We asked a nationally representative sampling of over one thousand Americans:

- What issues concern you?
- What kind of leaders do you seek?

The results literally set the agenda for this book.

THE QUEST FOR SOLUTIONS

Having determined the problems, we set to work finding solutions. We sought the widest possible array of approaches to the issues raised by Americans. To study the top public-policy research:

- We consulted with policy experts.
- We digested think-tank papers.
- We surveyed academic literature.
- We listened to advocacy groups.

And for each issue, we narrowed the number of solutions down to a finite number—each based on a different philosophical approach—and prepared an executive brief on each issue.

THE EXECUTIVE SEARCH

Once we determined what Americans want in their leaders, we sought out a new president, using the professional, proven method most major corporations use to find their leaders:

- We devised a detailed job description.
- We pinpointed attributes candidates should possess.
- We commissioned a "headhunter" to find candidates.

THE NATIONAL REFERENDUM _____

Our research had revealed a range of solutions to the nation's press-ing problems; our search had found a slate of potential leaders.
 Finally, we put it all to a vote.
 We asked a sampling of Americans to choose among the leaders we'd found and the solutions we'd concocted. And the result is the closest reflection yet devised of how Americans themselves would solve their problems.

PUTTING THE PROCESS IN MOTION

How do you start a revolution?
 The American Revolution didn't start with a public opinion poll.
 And neither did ours.
 It started with groups of concerned people with common beliefs join-ing together and expressing their concerns.
 And so did ours.
 Our quest to restore America wouldn't begin with a panel of experts. It began with a roomful of average citizens. To start listening to the voices of Americans, we began with the most American and democratic of fo-rums—a town hall.
 Our group assembled in Hopkinton, Massachusetts, a small town of two thousand three hundred residents, half an hour's drive from Boston. Hopkinton offered a unique glimpse of America: We chose it because we wanted to return to the roots of American democracy, the New En-gland towns where town-hall meetings first became the cornerstone of our system two centuries ago. Hopkinton still resembles the places where America's first town-hall meetings took place—but in reality, its problems are much like those of the rest of America. On the surface, Hopkinton

has the pastoral feel of a typical New England town: a lush common, a white-steepled church, two large state parks. Beneath the surface, it is like much of America in the 1990s: that is, it is full of citizens whose belief in the American ideal is being shaken by the realities of contemporary America.

Americans have always been imbued with a sense that they share a special mission, a unique destiny. The American ethic has been not merely to survive, but to prevail.

No more.

When we asked this group of Americans to tell us their feelings about their country, they didn't talk about American greatness or how our way of life had defeated communism. They talked about survival—about what America must do if it is to survive as a place to raise a family, educate children, to pursue your dreams.

Anger

Frustration

Bitterness

Disillusionment

Fear

Those emotions dominated the town hall, as participants—regardless of ideology, age, or gender—grappled with the mounting crises facing the nation. The underlying message was a united demand for change— a deep insistence that the status quo simply won't do anymore.

THE BURNING ISSUES

The town-hall discussion didn't turn up theoretical hypotheses or rhetorical debate; it produced a demand for action. What arose from the discussion were six issues participants considered *so essential that they must be addressed and resolved at all costs.* These were not divisive ideological issues; they were matters that bring Americans together out of concern for their children's future, and the health and safety of their families.

A DEARTH OF LEADERS

What we heard:

"We have lost regard for leaders and heroes and exceptional people."

—A forty-three-year-old male lawyer

The most profoundly expressed concern was that the nation's leaders had failed—that a new generation of leaders with a new set of ideals is needed. The disappointment in the people who lead was combined with an erosion of trust in the nation's governing institutions.

DECLINING SCHOOLS

What we heard:

"People have to understand that if you do not educate children today to function ten or fifteen years from now, there isn't going to be anybody paying your taxes, keeping you on social security and keeping us going."

—A thirty-seven-year-old teacher and mother

Changing and improving the nation's schools was on everyone's mind. The town-hall participants made it the first priority for immediate action. In fact, many said, all other changes are dependent on our ability to save our schools.

UNSAFE NEIGHBORHOODS

What we heard:

"How many of us won't drive in certain areas? How many of us worry about our children even going on a field trip?"

—A forty-year-old secretary

Even in the bucolic, solidly middle class, Norman Rockwell setting of Hopkinton, fear of crime is a central concern. Many participants expressed anger that those who commit crimes are not punished more severely.

POOR HEALTH CARE

What we heard:

"I see children aren't getting immunizations. Pregnant women are not getting nutrition. That doesn't make sense."

—A twenty-seven-year-old nurse

Participants were enraged at the state of health care in America. They called it unfair and they expressed fear for themselves and for poorer people who might not have adequate health coverage. Many said it was time for a national health-care system.

THE AILING ECONOMY

What we heard:

> "Future generations will not have it as well off as we do now."
>
> —*A fifty-eight-year-old contractor*

Many spoke their minds about their bleak perceptions and expectations of the national economy. Again and again, they bemoaned the nation's increasing unemployment, and the long, gradual decline of American industries compared to their Japanese and German counterparts.

THE SCOURGE OF DRUGS

What we heard:

> "Drugs, alcohol, and our youth. That's what I worry about."
>
> —*A forty-two-year-old homemaker*

Even in Hopkinton—far from the crack houses and drug gangs of the inner city—the fear of drugs has crept into the fabric of life. But people's major concern isn't combatting Colombian cocaine cartels, but simply keeping their children safe.

A NATIONAL TOWN HALL

Are the concerns of one town the concerns of all Americans?

With that question in mind, we constructed a national forum to determine the top concerns facing people throughout the country.

Building on what we heard at Hopkinton—and a look at polls from the past twenty years—we asked a national, random sampling of one thousand adult Americans to rank their most prominent concerns.

These issues would constitute the People's Agenda. They are the issues Americans consider to be the most pressing—the concerns that need to be addressed *now*.

Rank	Problem	Percentage of Americans who consider it "very important"
1.	The Economy	78
2.	Leadership	67
3.	The Deficit	66
4.	Education	65
5.	Crime	65
6.	AIDS	62
7.	Drugs	60
8.	Affordable Health Care	52
9.	The Environment	47
10.	Abortion	39
11.	Homelessness	38
12.	Poverty	38
13.	Sexual Discrimination/Harassment	37
14.	Race	35
15.	Gun Control	30

Regardless of ideology—liberal, conservative, or something in between—Americans agree on the preeminence of these issues. Though they differ on approaches to solving the problems, there's little disagreement that these are the matters that the nation simply must resolve.

PART I: WHO SHOULD LEAD US?

Whatever the agenda, it won't be addressed properly without proper direction from the top. Yet our electoral process—with its sound-bite campaigns and horse-race media coverage—seems to fail us again and again.

What do Americans want in a leader? We found out, and then we conducted the most exacting search in history to find a president. In our detailed national referendum, we determined the specific characteristics Americans want in their leaders. And then we took it a step further. We turned over the specifications to one of the nation's top executive search firms, and gave them their most challenging assignment to date: to come up with a list of leaders who fit the bill. We'll reveal the list of these leaders for the nineties and beyond.

And once we've got the people in place, what should their agenda be? In three sections, we'll tackle the problems facing America.

PART II: SOLVE-AT-ALL-COSTS ISSUES

How should we save the national economy from the brink of disaster?

What can we do to reform our schools and bring them up to the standards of the world's leading industrial nations?

Should America revamp its health-care system to provide wider access to care?

How can we curb rising rates of crime and make our neighborhoods safe again?

Why does the scourge of drug use continue unabated—and is there hope of bringing the drug problem under control?

In Part II of this book, we address these five issues—the social problems Americans have indicated are the most pressing, most immediate concerns. These are survival issues—problems that absolutely must be dealt with.

For each issue, we'll discuss, listen—and then decide what to do.

Each chapter will introduce an issue, then examine several solutions proposed by academic, political, and policy experts. A list of the most prominent options has been voted on by a nationally representative sampling of Americans.

PART III: ISSUES OF SACRIFICE AND COMMITMENT

No one is in favor of poverty, or homelessness. Everyone wants a clean environment and we all yearn for a cure for AIDS. Certainly, nearly all Americans agree that the rising national deficit ought to be brought under control.

But we can't agree on the details. How much attention should we pay to these matters? How much should we sacrifice? How much should we spend?

Part III of this book will examine issues on which Americans generally agree in principle, but disagree widely in terms of commitment.

How much effort should be put into these issues? We used our comprehensive referendum process to measure the real level of commitment—the price Americans will pay to solve these problems.

PART IV: WEDGE ISSUES

Abortion. Sexual discrimination and harassment. Racial division. Gun control.

These and similar issues are causing wide division and polarization in the American social fabric. Wedge issues are hotly debated in the media, highlighting the strains and differences within our society—yet Americans continue to differ sharply on these matters.

Though these issues polarize the nation and its political debate, most Americans don't have clear black-and-white positions on these questions. Politicians and the media have presented the options as stark choices between two absolute extremes.

In Part IV, in a national referendum we'll allow Americans to address these issues not as simplistic, yes-or-no questions, but as highly complex, shadowy dilemmas.

Our goal is not to divide further, but to find—in the cacophony of voices—common strains. We'll work to forge a middle ground, setting the groundwork to forge a new consensus on these vexing issues.

TAPPING INTO AMERICA

This isn't a public opinion poll. It's a vision of the future.

Once we'd gathered the consensus about which issues should get top priority, it was time to set a course of action.

How did we move from identifying problems to finding solutions? The details—the results—will be revealed in the pages that follow.

This project is a first. Certainly, the media is filled with attempts to gauge American opinion: political polls, market surveys, demographic studies. But this is the first time that so many Americans have been asked to identify so many pressing problems—and then to *solve* them. We simply asked Americans for their help. And the response overwhelmed us.

TIME TO ACT

For too long, these questions have smoldered, while the nation stood by waiting for answers. We've had politics. We've had rhetoric. We've had media. We've had presidents come and go. But we haven't had solutions.

Now we do. The people have spoken. Listen to them, and amid the despair, you'll hear conviction. Amid the decline, you'll hear hope. Amid the division, you'll hear unity.

America is ready to fix itself.

Just listen.

★

I
WHO SHOULD
LEAD US?

★

What if we could choose the best person to lead the country?

Not the best politician. Not the guy who can quote the most economic statistics off the top of his head. Not the best guest on *Larry King Live.*

Just the best leader. Period. The best person to take charge and bring America back to greatness.

What if we could do that?

We can. And we will—in this chapter.

You've heard it before: They just don't make leaders like they used to. Like Jefferson. Like Lincoln. Like Franklin Roosevelt.

But they do. We looked. And—you'll be amazed—we found them.

It's not the American people who have been lacking. It's not the electorate. It's the way we choose our leaders. Whatever presidential campaigns have become in the 1990s, almost everyone agrees that they're not working. They're not letting the best people rise to the top. And we all—those of us who vote—trudge off to the polls, without enthusiasm, and cast our ballots for the least objectionable candidate.

With all the brains and talent in this country, that seems ludicrous.

We wanted to let *the people* speak. Not the media. Not the party chiefs. Not special interests.

And here was the lesson: if you leave it up to the people, the system works. We listened to what Americans want in a president. And then we went out and found people—proven leaders—to meet *their* specifications. We found that there are leaders out there just waiting to be discovered. We found seven people who would make dynamic, thoughtful, intelligent leaders for the nineties. The kind of leaders people really want. We were astounded. And when you meet them, you will be too.

WHAT HAPPENED TO OUR LEADERS?

Before we set out to find new leaders, we asked: Why are we so disenchanted with the leaders we've got now? Poll after poll shows that Americans feel that their leaders have lost touch with them. In the twenty years since Watergate, the nation has lost faith in the presidency and the Congress—not the people in office, but the very *institutions* of power.

In fact, two-thirds of Americans believe the quality of the nation's political leaders is worsening.

And that plummeting confidence extends beyond politics to nearly every sector of public life. In the past two decades, Americans have lost faith in organized religion, in labor unions, in corporations, in banks and (understandably) savings and loans.

Combined with the loss of faith is a loss of *hope*. We can't find outstanding individuals to lead us out of this mess. The crisis of leadership belies a void in the fabric of American society: Americans simply don't have anyone to look up to anymore.

NO LEADERS

- Two in three Americans don't believe we have any leaders with the ability to address the nation's ills.

NO ROLE MODELS

- Half of Americans don't have anyone in their family they'd like to model themselves after.

NO HEROES

- Seventy percent of Americans believe our nation doesn't have heroes anymore.

Where are the heroes of the past—the idols whose untarnished profiles dominated the American cultural landscape? Earlier in the century, heroes like Babe Ruth, Charles Lindbergh, and Joe Louis captured the nation's attention and its unflagging respect. Eleanor Roosevelt became a role model to millions of women. In the 1930s and '40s, Joe DiMaggio represented an American ideal: a man of deeds rather than words. In the 1960s, Rev. Dr. Martin Luther King, Jr., stirred the nation with his courage and conviction.

And now? *Americans just don't believe in anything strongly enough to be impressed by its attainment.*

Why? Because of a dearth of leadership. But the right leadership exists. And—as you'll see—we found it.

WHAT DO WE WANT FROM OUR LEADERS?

We were prodded on in our search by our conversations with Americans. When we asked them their concerns, again and again they pleaded for thoughtful, strong individuals to step forward to positions of importance.

Leadership. "People don't want to lead," one woman complained. "Those who really have the intelligence and the drive, they're doing other things, and I think that maybe we have lost that regard for leaders and heroes and exceptional people."

A different perspective. Said one man: "That's the frustrating part for me: looking for a national leader who can break through and say, 'Hey, I might not have all the answers, but I'm going to give you a different perspective on what we should be doing.'"

Vision. And what do Americans want in their leaders? "We want someone who's competent, intelligent, and has a vision," said another woman. "We're asking for someone to plan our futures, and the futures of our children."

CANDIDATES MISS THE MARK

While Americans clearly perceive a lack of leadership, those who seek to direct the nation underestimate the significance of the nation's yearning for authoritative, enlightened standard-bearers. Campaigns for high office have come to focus on *ideology* and *new ideas* and the details of issues. Yet Americans place a much higher priority on a candidate's capacity for *leadership.*

AMERICANS WANT LEADERS, NOT POLICY WONKS

- What qualities are important in choosing a president?
  - Thirty-six percent of voters in one poll said leadership; 4 percent cited new ideas.[1]
  - In another survey, 51 percent said leadership, while 3 percent mentioned ideology.[2]

- When asked what attributes they seek in political candidates, 24 percent said leadership, 15 percent said intelligence, and 10 percent mentioned decisiveness.[3]

HOW HAVE OUR PRESIDENTS STACKED UP AS LEADERS?

We're going to introduce you to the leaders of the future. But to find them, we had to look first to the past—to how presidents have stacked up as leaders.

What gives one politician the aura of authority and vision, while others come off as inconsistent, weak, or merely ineffectual? And what makes the public's perception of a candidate's leadership qualities waver and shift?

We know more about how to choose the most appropriate next president by examining the leadership ratings of the past three presidents.

JIMMY CARTER: GOOD ISN'T GOOD ENOUGH _____

Americans came to perceive Jimmy Carter as a highly ethical man without the capacity to lead the nation.

In the 1976 election—in the wake of Watergate—Americans considered moral leadership (41 percent) as important in choosing a presidential candidate as fixing the economy (40 percent).[4] Throughout the campaign, Jimmy Carter held a consistent 12-percent edge over Gerald Ford in perception of leadership. Carter defeated Ford in large part because he was perceived to be a stronger leader.

But during his troubled presidency, Americans came to question Carter's capacity for leadership. The proportion of Americans who considered him to have strong leadership qualities fell precipitously:

- February 1977: 70 percent
- October 1977: 62 percent
- July 1978: 36 percent

In fact, Americans continued to hold Carter in high esteem. Seventy-six percent said he was "a man of high moral principles," and 69 percent said he was "intelligent." But 67 percent said he lacked "strong leadership qualities."

RONALD REAGAN: TOPPING THE CHARTS

Remarkably, Ronald Reagan's image as a leader was so strong that he left office with leadership ratings as high as when he came to power.

In the summer of 1980, the pundits and pollsters said the fall election was too close to call. In retrospect, the leadership ratings proved a strong predictor that the electorate would opt for Ronald Reagan.

The leadership gap:

- June 1980: Reagan led 57 percent to 26 percent in leadership rating.
- September 1980: Reagan led 65 percent to 31 percent.

Through most of the campaign, Carter led in preference polls as he trailed in leadership perception. At the polls, however, Americans voted for the candidate they perceived as a better leader.

Unlike Carter's, Reagan's leadership marks never waned.

- *Early ratings.* In 1982, his leadership rating hovered at 60 percent.
- *The first term.* In February 1984, as he was preparing for his reelection campaign, his rating stood at 76 percent.
- *Reelection campaign.* In a 1984 poll, 60 percent said Reagan was a better leader; 22 percent preferred Walter Mondale, his Democratic opponent.
- *Leaving office.* In January 1988, 66 percent of Americans gave him an excellent or good rating in leadership qualities.

GEORGE BUSH: LEADERSHIP EBB AND FLOW

In contrast to Carter's headlong plunge and Reagan's steady climb, George Bush's leadership image rode a roller coaster. His marks as a leader rose and fell, depending on events and his reaction to them.

- In October 1987, when he was vice president, only 46 percent of Americans thought Bush had the leadership qualities a president requires.

- By the 1988 election, his leadership ratings had risen to a respectable 65 percent.
- One year into his term, Bush's leadership marks had plunged to 53 percent.
- In May of 1991, in the full glow of his success as Commander in Chief in the Gulf War, his leadership ratings soared to a stratospheric 86 percent.
- By late August 1992, with the economy on a steady decline, more Americans thought Bush had done a poor job of providing strong leadership (49 percent) than thought he had done a good job (45 percent).[5]

In fact, by October 1992, nearly three in four Americans felt the time had come for a new generation of leadership to cope with new problems and opportunities. Enter Bill Clinton.

WHAT, EXACTLY, IS LEADERSHIP?

As we set out to find the best possible leader for America, we paused to ask what, exactly, we were looking for.

Leadership is hard to define, but easy to recognize. It is not ideology, technical competence, knowledge, or ideas. It is a combination of vision, team building, motivating, and inspiring sacrifice.

Projecting a vision. A leader must have a vision for the future. That vision must be backed by strategies.

And a leader is more than a manager. Says John P. Kotter, a Harvard Business School professor: *Managers execute orders and cope with the complexity of organizations; leaders face challenges and cause change.*

Building a team. Having set forth such a vision, a leader must create coalitions of people committed to put that plan into action.

Says management expert Ralph Stayer: *Managers form committees; leaders build teams.* The difference: While a committee has agendas, a team has a collective vision.

Motivating followers. Once leaders have established teams, they motivate their followers to move in the direction they have set. In the words of Harry Truman: *Leaders motivate by "getting men to do what they don't want to do and like it."*

According to David R. Palmer, superintendent of West Point, leaders motivate most effectively by promising fairness in reward and sacrifice. "If you are not fair and are not willing to sacrifice personally, you will be seen as self-serving by those who follow you."

Inspiring sacrifice. All true leadership involves asking something of those who would follow.

Peter Kreeft, professor of philosophy at Boston College, asserts that America needs leaders who combine all of these elements, starting with solid visions for the country. *"To be a leader,"* he says, *"you have to lead people to a goal worth having—something that's really good and really there."*

ARE THERE LEADERS OUT THERE SOMEWHERE?

With full recognition of the dearth of leaders—and the importance of vision and leadership—in mind, we set our process in motion:

WE SET OUT TO HIRE A NEW PRESIDENT _____

But our process would have none of the pitfalls of modern-day election-eering, with its sound-bite campaigning, smear tactics, and sloganeering.

Our process was simple: we recognized the need; we defined the challenge; and we set out to fill the vacancy.

Our goal: to hire a president the way successful corporations fill executive positions:

- *The Questions.* First, we asked a cross section of Americans what *specific qualities* they seek in a president.
- *The Job.* We took the information they gave us and created a job description.
- *The Experts.* We turned over that ideal profile to a leading executive search firm.
- *The List.* The search firm came up with an extensive list of candidates, which we narrowed to a short list.
- *The Vote.* We submitted the slate of nominees to a group of Americans.

- *The Choice.* Our group of citizens cast their ballots and chose the best candidate for president.

DO WE KNOW WHAT WE SEEK IN A LEADER?

Before we started our search, we had to know: What do Americans want in a president? To answer this question, we interviewed a random national sampling of over one thousand Americans. Each person looked at a detailed list of seventy-four leadership traits.

The question: How important is each quality in deciding whether an individual has the essential leadership characteristics to be president? Our group of Americans ranked each item from "1" (not important at all) to "7" (an absolute must). With the results collected, we ranked the attributes in descending order, by the percentage of "7" responses.

Rank	Leadership Attribute	Percentage Who Rate It a Must
1.	Honesty	79
2.	Good judgment in crisis	75
3.	Trustworthiness	70
4.	Common sense	69
5.	Intelligence	68
6.	Knowledge	64
7.	Puts country's interests ahead of politics	63
8.	Knows where he/she stands on issues	62
9.	Credibility/believability	61
10.	Ability to get things done	60
	Integrity	60
12.	Understands complex issues	56
	Patriotism	56
14.	Has defined plan for moving nation ahead	55
15.	A team builder	53
16.	A motivator	52
	Self-confidence	52
18.	Sincerity	51
19.	Decisiveness	50
20.	Sees office as high duty, not achievement	49

21.	Take-charge person	48
	Open-mindedness	48
23.	Administrative competence	47
24.	Capacity to articulate vision	46
	Sense of fairness	46

The list makes it clear that Americans have a sophisticated and comprehensive idea of what they want in a president. The list clusters around seven fundamental qualities:

THE PEOPLE'S LEADERSHIP PROFILE (THE SEVEN C'S)

1. Character
2. Competence
3. Commitment
4. Confidence
5. Clarity
6. Compassion
7. Charisma

SPECIALIZED LEADERS

Our objective wasn't to find superhumans who embody fully all seven of these categories. *Most leaders really embody just one or two particular aspects of leadership.* (Reagan, the loyal conservative, embodied clarity of position; Carter excelled in the character issues.) And the type of leader that's best for the country depends on the times.

HOLD ON JUST A SECOND. . .

Before we launched our hunt for leaders, we cleared away some long-held assumptions about what sort of person the president ought to be.

SHOULD MR. SMITH GO TO WASHINGTON? _____

Some of our greatest presidents have risen to power with relatively little experience as professional politicians. The nation's appetite is growing for political outsiders—people free from the existing quagmire of government.

HOW ABOUT MS. SMITH? _____

Women, comprising 51 percent of the population, are the untapped resource in American politics. Why? Polls have shown that Americans neither value nor admire leadership characteristics in women—the very same qualities they seek in men.

- A study shows that 40 percent of men admire leadership qualities in men, while 10 percent admire them in women.[6]

And research from our previous book, *The Day America Told the Truth*, shows that both men and women agree that women are morally superior to men: more honest, more caring, harder working, less violent.[7] As the 1992 election showed, Americans are at last recognizing that a great wellspring of leadership exists among women.

NOBODY LIKES A KNOW-IT-ALL _____

Americans don't want an encyclopedia; they want a leader. It would be better if the candidate was a generalist, rather than a technician of the issues. Vision supersedes specific expertise.

AN MBA AT THE TOP? _____

Does the president need to be a problem-solving managerial type? No. A good leader can employ all the professional managers he or she needs on the White House staff. Managers should execute policy, while it's the job of a leader to set forth vision and direction.

WHAT'S THE JOB DESCRIPTION?

Imagine the want ad:

> Wanted: President for large North American democracy. No experience
> necessary. Send résumé, vision.

We had the advice of leadership experts. We had the lessons of the past. And we had the most important information of all: the people's specs. They all combined to make the picture of the ideal president. Here's the list of attributes we created to turn over to our search team:

- *Visionary.* Americans want a leader with a program, with direction, and with a view to the future. Above all, people want to be led by a visionary.

- *Articulate.* Even the greatest plan is irrelevant if the American people don't understand it. The president should have the capacity to communicate in a way that moves people to action. Presidents like Jefferson, Lincoln, Franklin Roosevelt, and John F. Kennedy showed the power of rhetorical poetry—a president's ability to speak spontaneously and with eloquence.

- *Inspiring.* A leader doesn't accomplish goals alone, but rather inspires followers to work together toward a common goal. The candidate ought to have the ability to be fair in rewarding excellence and demanding sacrifices.

- *Able to delegate.* The most successful presidents in history delegated authority skillfully. The failures were crippled by overwork and bureaucracy.

  To delegate effectively, the president needs people. To that end, the president must have a record of forging close-knit teams that work together toward a common purpose.

- *Moral.* The president should be a person of the highest moral principles and of sound character.

- *Compassionate.* Like Lincoln, the president should be a person of great compassion, a leader who feels the hopes, fears, dreams, and dreads of all the people.

- *Patriotic.* Duty, not ambition, should be the factor spurring the president to serve in high office. To paraphrase Woodrow Wilson, the leader's goal should be to do something, not to be somebody.

- *Courageous.* The president ought to have the ability to follow his or her convictions, whatever the political price—to do what is best, not what is most expedient.

HOW DID WE SET OUT TO FIND THE IDEAL PRESIDENT?

Given Americans' growing discontent with their leaders, we made it our mission to seek leadership in nontraditional sources—to look far beyond the customary ranks of senators and representatives.

WE BROUGHT IN THE PROS _____

Imagine an efficient, methodical, comprehensive, and *effective* way to find a president.

We found it. And it worked.

How do America's most successful corporations choose their leaders? They have come to rely on executive search firms, companies that have made a specialty of looking far and wide for exactly the right person to fit a job.

And so did we.

We enlisted the help of Gilbert Tweed Associates, a respected firm with twenty years of experience in finding CEOs, presidents, and directors for corporate America. The firm's clients include Coca-Cola, Xerox, General Electric, and *The New York Times*.

THE ASSIGNMENT: FIND A PRESIDENT _____

We turned over the "people's specs" for president of the United States. And Gilbert Tweed's team of fifty researchers went to work:

- They started in the most obvious places, reviewing the qualifications of:
    - All 436 members of Congress.
    - All 50 U.S. governors.
    - The top 50 U.S. mayors.
- They scoured the business world, assessing the abilities of the chief executive officers of:
    - The top 20 manufacturing corporations.

- - The top 20 banks.
  - The top 20 communications and media companies.
- They turned their focus to other institutions that serve the public, seeking leadership among:
  - Curators of the top cultural institutions.
  - Heads of the top arts organizations.
  - Chief executives of the top nonprofit and charitable concerns.
  - Presidents of the best universities.
- And they looked at every White House Fellowship recipient since 1965.

In all, they carefully assessed the qualifications of nearly one thousand contenders.

The research team compared the talents and strengths of each candidate to the specific criteria our research had concocted. And through that process, they narrowed the list to 90 potential candidates:

THE FIELD OF 90

Corporate America	Affiliation
John H. Bryan	CEO, Sara Lee Corp.
Wayne Calloway	CEO, PepsiCo
Robert Crandall	President, American Airlines
Michael Eisner	President, Walt Disney Co.
Stan Gault	Chairman, Goodyear Tire and Rubber
Edward Lawrence Hennessy	Chairman/CEO Allied Signal
Lee Iaccoca	Former CEO, Chrysler Corp.
Reggie Lewis	CEO, Beatrice Foods
John Francis McGillicuddy	Manufacturers Hanover Trust
Charles Hewes Moore	ITW Finishing Systems
Ross Perot	Founder, EDS
Peter Ueberroth	Former Commissioner of Major League Baseball
Roy Vagelos, M.D.	President and CEO, Merck & Co.
Jack Welch	CEO, General Electric
Clifton Wharton	Chairman, TIAA CREF

Mayors	City
Emanuel Cleaver II	Kansas City
Richard M. Daley	Chicago
Raymond Flynn	Boston (former)

Donald M. Fraser	Minneapolis
James D. Griffin	Buffalo
Sharon Pratt Kelly	Washington
Louis Saavedra	Albuquerque
Kurt L. Schmoke	Baltimore
Vincent Schoemehl	St. Louis
Dwight Tillery	Cincinnati
Wellington E. Webb	Denver

Governors	**State**
John David Ashcroft	Missouri
Rafael Hernandez Colon	Puerto Rico
Ann Richards	Texas
Howard Dean, M.D.	Vermont
Barbara Roberts	Oregon
Pete Wilson	California

Senators	**State**
David Boren	Oklahoma
Bill Bradley	New Jersey
Thomas Daschle	South Dakota
Dianne Feinstein	California
Jake Garn	Utah
Philip Gramm	Texas
Daniel Inouye	Hawaii
Howard Metzenbaum	Ohio
George Mitchell	Maine
Barbara Mikulski	Maryland
Edmund Muskie	Maine (former)
Warren Rudman	New Hampshire (former)
Paul Tsongas	Massachusetts

Congressional Representatives	**State**
Ben Nighthorse Campbell	Colorado
Ada Deer	Wisconsin
Byron L. Dorgan	North Dakota
Eleanor Holmes Norton	District of Columbia (Delegate)
Olympia Snowe	Maine

Educators	**Affiliation**
Barbara Jordan	University of Texas
Rosabeth Moss Kantor	Harvard University
Philip Crosby	Philip Crosby Associates

James Freedman	Dartmouth College
Vartan Gregorian	Brown University
Dr. Sheldon Hackney	University of Pennsylvania
Guy McKeen	Former President, Yale University
James Q. Wilson	UCLA

Law	**Affiliation**
Yvonne Braithwaite Burke	Former U.S. Representative
Hillary Clinton	Arkansas lawyer, First Lady
Vernon Jordan	Akin, Gump, Straus, Haven & Field
Elliot Richardson	Former U.S. Attorney General

Government and Politics	**Affiliation**
Lamar Alexander	Former Secretary of Education
James Baker III	Former Secretary of State
Griffin B. Bell	Former U.S. Attorney General
Ron Brown	Secretary of Commerce
Jimmy Carter	Former President
Richard Cheney	Former Secretary of Defense
Henry Cisneros	Secretary of Housing and Urban Development
Molly Joel Coye	Department of Health
Alan Greenspan	Former Chairman, Federal Reserve Bank
Marlene Johnson	Former Lieutenant Governor, Minnesota
David Kearns	Former Undersecretary of Education
Jack Kemp	Former Secretary of Housing and Urban Development
Jeanne Kirkpatrick	Former UN Ambassador
C. Everett Koop	Former Surgeon General
Marvin Runyon	Postmaster General
Gen. Norman Schwartzkopf	U.S. Army, retired
Dale Schoettler	State Treasurer, Colorado
Donna Shalala	Secretary of Health and Human Services
Louis Sullivan	Former Secretary of Health and Human Services
Gen. Colin Powell	Former Chairman, Joint Chiefs of Staff

Miscellaneous	**Affiliation**
Elizabeth Dole	President, American Red Cross
Marian Wright Edelman	President, Children's Defense Fund
Thomas Hoving	Former Curator, Metropolitan Museum
Charles Murray	Author
Ralph Nader	Consumer Advocate

Leon Shenandoah	Head Chief, Onondaga Nation
Franklyn Thomas	President, Ford Foundation
Faye Wadelton	Former Head, Planned Parenthood

REALITY CHECK: THE PROVEN FAILURES

Why didn't some prominent names make the cut?

In short: Our leaders don't measure up. Getting into office doesn't make you a leader.

Perhaps the most revealing conclusion of our search process was that many of the figures who have ascended to national office—or run high-profile campaigns—simply don't fulfill the standards of leadership Americans gave us. They're politicians, but by the people's standards, they're not good leaders.

- *Former President George Bush* lacked the "vision thing"—he never articulated a strong, clear sense of purpose.
- *Former Vice President Dan Quayle* is missing the competence and character Americans seek in true leaders.
- *Sen. Paul Tsongas* is a bright and articulate visionary, but doesn't have the charisma and clarity of message Americans say they require.
- *Ross Perot*, an effective and popular heckler, a thorn in the side of establishment politicians, has never shown the more positive leadership ability that Americans seek. (He made our preliminary list, but was eliminated early.)
- *President Clinton* mastered the electoral process, but fails to meet Americans' leadership standards. By objective assessment, he falls short on the integrity scale, and his mediocre leadership ratings show that Americans don't perceive him as a strong leader.

NARROWING THE FIELD

With 90 remaining candidates, the search team condensed the criteria. It distilled our Seven C's—the seven characteristics of strong leaders—to three overarching qualities:

- Integrity (character and compassion)
- Vision (commitment and clarity)
- Leadership (charisma, confidence, and competence)

As the team made the cut, it was careful to avoid any sort of bias. The goal was to create a list including:

- Roughly equal numbers of liberals, moderates, and conservatives
- Representatives of business, education, law, and public service
- Both sexes, and various races and ethnic backgrounds

The team reviewed each candidate by each category, giving scores from 1 to 10. After much analysis, reanalysis, and soul-searching, the team assembled its rankings, and narrowed the list to eighteen candidates:

John Bryan, President and CEO, Sara Lee Corp.

Emanuel Cleaver II, Mayor of Kansas City, Missouri

Howard Dean, M.D., Governor of Vermont

Elizabeth Dole, President, American Red Cross

Marian Wright Edelman, President, Children's Defense Fund

Michael Eisner, Chairman and CEO, Walt Disney Co.

Daniel Inouye, U.S. Senator, Hawaii

Barbara Jordan, Professor, LBJ School of Public Affairs

Jack Kemp, Former U.S. Secretary of Housing and Urban
    Development

George Mitchell, U.S. Senate Majority Leader

Gen. Colin Powell, Former Chairman, Joint Chiefs of Staff

Elliot Richardson, Former U.S. Attorney General

Ann Richards, Governor of Texas

Warren Rudman, Former U.S. Senator, New Hampshire

Donna Shalala, U.S. Secretary of Health and Human Services

Pete Wilson, Governor of California

Roy Vagelos, M.D., President and CEO, Merck & Co.

John F. Welch, Jr., President and CEO, General Electric

THE SHORT LIST

The goal of the process was to submit an even shorter list of options to our cross section of the electorate—a list manageable enough so that those making the decision would maintain energy and interest in the process. We wanted our sampling of voters to put serious thought into the sort of leader they want, so we worked to narrow the list to seven.

With that objective, we and our search team gave serious consideration to each of the eighteen candidates, and to the variety of individuals included on the slate. The search team considered each of the individuals on the list of eighteen, giving close scrutiny to (a) all of the leadership qualities, (b) professional track record, and (c) creating a final slate that offers a wide variety of choices, across a spectrum of ethnic backgrounds, professional fields, political outlooks, and previous government experience. Together, we came up with a list offering a range of experience, background, and perspective.

- Three are women.
- Two are business leaders.
- Two are educators.
- Two are members of minority groups.
- Three are experienced politicians.
- One is a physician.

THE SLATE

Here, then, are the finalists:
- *John Bryan,* the president and CEO of the Sara Lee Corporation.
- *Barbara Jordan,* the civil rights activist and professor at the Lyndon Baines Johnson School of Public Affairs.
- *Jack Kemp,* the former U.S. secretary of housing and urban development.

- *Ann Richards,* the popular and outspoken governor of Texas.
- *Warren Rudman,* the former Republican senator from New Hampshire.
- *Donna Shalala,* the U.S. secretary of health and human services.
- *Roy Vagelos, M.D.,* the president and CEO of Merck & Co., the pharmaceutical manufacturer.

THE ENVELOPE, PLEASE

Until now, shallow, sound-bite politics has come to dominate the process of choosing our presidents. We sought to offer an alternative.

To help our two thousand Americans make their choices, we provided a brief look at the candidates—who they are, what they've done, and what they hope to accomplish.

THE PROGRESSIVE EXECUTIVE _____

JOHN H. BRYAN, JR.
PRESIDENT AND CHIEF EXECUTIVE
   OFFICER, SARA LEE
   CORPORATION
BORN: OCTOBER 5, 1936, WEST
   POINT, MISSISSIPPI

What would a shrewd chieftain of corporate America bring to the White House? In John H. Bryan, Jr.'s case, a personality born of southern geniality, a zealous business acumen, and an innate progressive social consciousness.

Bryan didn't work his way to the top. When he was twenty-three, his father put him at the helm of the family's meat processing business, the largest employer in West Point, Mississippi, a town of eight thousand. He later sold the company to Consolidated Foods—now Sara Lee Corp.— where he quickly rose to become chief executive officer. He presides over one of the nation's fifty largest corporations, with a diverse empire including Hanes underwear, Kiwi shoe care products, L'eggs panty hose, Jimmy Dean smoked meats, and Kitchens of Sara Lee.

With a sense of social responsibility imbued by his mother—an ardent New Dealer who worked to improve the plight of the disabled and the elderly—Bryan has consistently used his position as a business leader to advocate change and social justice. In the midst of the social strife of the 1960s South, he was an outspoken advocate for civil rights as chairman of the local school board and president of the chamber of commerce. He was the first employer in his hometown to do away with the vestiges of segregation—separate drinking fountains and rest rooms—and to put African-Americans in supervisory positions. When West Point closed its public schools to avoid integration, he joined blacks in suing the town, and when the district reopened, Bryan (who is white) sent his four children to predominantly black schools. When the city council bulldozed the public swimming pool in 1964 for fear that the federal government would order its integration, Bryan borrowed $26,000 from an Alabama bank to build a pool that black residents could use.

To this day, he remains active in promoting progressive issues. Sara Lee sends 2 percent of its pretax profits to charitable causes, many of them groups that aid the poor and disadvantaged. He's active in the Urban League, and Bryan has been a strong advocate for working women, chairing Catalyst, an organization dedicated to advancing the status of women in the workplace. He has spread his social conscious- ness to his employees: Sara Lee requires its managers to devote time to public service; the company gives time to spend volunteering in the com- munity.

Bryan is known as a formal, serious, and meticulous man with a gentle southern charm and an intensity and take-charge attitude. He has a long- time habit of scribbling notes to himself as he goes about his daily activ- ities, even on his days off; at night, he transfers the notes onto lists to plan his next day and week. He has a keen interest in global affairs, acquiring knowledge that has served him well in his successful international ex- pansion of Sara Lee to markets in Europe and Asia over the past decade.

A descendant of Thomas Jefferson, Bryan is a political maverick—a lifelong registered Democrat who has voted for GOP presidential candidates as often as for members of his own party.

THE ARTICULATE CONSCIENCE

BARBARA JORDAN
PROFESSOR, LYNDON BAINES
JOHNSON SCHOOL OF PUBLIC
AFFAIRS, UNIVERSITY OF TEXAS
BORN: FEBRUARY 21, 1936,
HOUSTON, TEXAS

The "horizon of gender equity is limitless," Barbara Jordan told the Democratic National Convention in the summer of 1992. "And what we see today is simply a dress rehearsal for the day and time we meet in convention to nominate Madam President."

When that day and time come, Barbara Jordan might well be the woman who should be making the acceptance speech. An eloquent, tireless advocate for society's disenfranchised, a model of ethics in government, and a singular, independent thinker, Jordan is the sort of unfaltering character who could bring unwavering respect to the White House.

Jordan's strong empathy for the nation's impoverished stems from her own background. The youngest of three daughters from a poor family in a Houston ghetto, she overcame her impoverished youth to attend college and law school. Jordan twice ran unsuccessfully for the Texas House of Representatives, but in 1966, she won election to the state senate, the first African-American ever elected to the Texas Legislature.

She consistently worked for those without a voice, backing proposals to increase the minimum wage, extend social security benefits to homemakers, provide legal services for the poor, and expand programs aiding the elderly and the sick.

Her work gave Jordan a solid reputation in the state, and in 1972, she became the first African-American elected to Congress from the South since Reconstruction.

During the televised Watergate hearings in the summer of 1974, Jordan—previously little known—made a name for herself with her articulate testimonial on the value of the Constitution. "My faith in the Constitution is whole," she said. "It is complete. It is total. I am not going to sit here and be an idle spectator to the diminution, the subversion, the destruction of the Constitution."[8]

A civil rights activist, she has also remained an independent and pragmatic politician, making an effort not to focus narrowly on the issues of African-Americans. Asked what type of leader the nation needs, she said: "Someone who speaks for *all* Americans without equivocation."

Jordan left politics in 1977, and is now a professor at the Lyndon Baines Johnson School of Public Affairs at the University of Texas at Austin. In 1991, Texas Governor Ann Richards appointed her as special counsel on ethics, and she remains an outspoken advocate of ethics in government.

"I absolutely believe politics is an honorable profession," she has said. "I wish more people would see politicians as public servants, because that's what they are."[9]

As for her own prospects in politics, Jordan has said little. In her teaching position, she sees herself as having a vital role in training the next generation of leaders. In 1988, she was diagnosed with multiple sclerosis, and she now uses a wheelchair for movement. Yet she retains a high profile and remains active and vital in party politics. And she remains one of the most articulate speakers on political issues. A prominent Texas journalist once compared speaking to Jordan with interviewing God.

Is she the type of leader America needs?

"It's not my turn," she once said. "When it's my turn, you'll know it."[10]

THE BLEEDING-HEART CONSERVATIVE _____

JACK KEMP
FORMER U.S. SECRETARY OF
    HOUSING AND URBAN
    DEVELOPMENT
BORN: JULY 13, 1935,
    LOS ANGELES, CALIFORNIA

"You don't go into a huddle and say, 'Has anybody got a good play?'"
Jack Kemp once said about leadership. "You take charge."[11]

The former pro quarterback has taken heed of his own advice, bringing his own set of ideas with him throughout his ascent in politics—as
aide to California Governor Ronald Reagan in the 1960s, as a member of
Congress, and as President George Bush's secretary of housing and urban
development. Kemp labels himself a "bleeding-heart conservative," a
steadfast backer of supply-side economics who seeks to use entrepre-
neurial capitalism as a tool to fight poverty.

An intellectual late bloomer, Kemp majored in physical education in
college, but has become known as a man of ideas who can quote esoteric
political philosophers and obscure economists. What makes him attractive as a leader is a combination of consensus-building and independence: Kemp builds coalitions around his ideas, yet he isn't toadying. As
HUD secretary, he was an occasional outspoken critic of the very administration he served.

Born in Los Angeles, where his father owned a small trucking business,
Kemp went on to become a professional football quarterback who led
the Buffalo Bills to two American Football League titles. He cofounded
the league's players' association, and worked to negotiate wage-and-
benefits packages for his colleagues. Late in his football career, then-
California Governor Ronald Reagan hired him in football's off-season as
a special assistant. He was elected to the U.S. House of Representatives

in 1970, serving a district in Buffalo. In Congress, Kemp became a consistent voice of neoconservatism, promoting the idea that the government's big-money Great Society programs of the 1960s themselves perpetuated poverty by discouraging hard work.

It was Kemp who encouraged President Reagan to adopt the supply-side economics, and his proposal was at the heart of Reagan's tax-cutting policies. Kemp saw himself as the heir to Reagan's economic philosophy—and leadership—but he failed in a 1988 primary bid to defeat George Bush, who later made him his housing secretary.

On the Cabinet, Kemp advocated a conservative "War on Poverty"—one that, unlike its liberal sixties namesake, would rely on conservative principles and promote what Kemp labels "empowerment" of the poor. He worked to establish inner-city free enterprise zones, where tax breaks would give the impoverished impetus to create small businesses. He advocated welfare reform to put the poor to work, and he promoted tenant management of public housing.

Kemp, a spirited public speaker, is so taken with his own ideas that he has become known for lengthy and overly enthusiastic speeches. He has made no secret of his desire to serve in the White House. But is he right for America? His supply-side ideas brought prosperity on the 1980s, followed by an extended economic slump. Yet he has adapted his "empowerment" package to face the crises of the nineties head-on. He brings a combination of ideas, experience, and iconoclasm that would serve well in the White House.

THE GOOD OL' GOVERNOR ⸻

ANN RICHARDS
GOVERNOR OF TEXAS
BORN: SEPTEMBER 1, 1922,
  WACO, TEXAS

"I have always used humor to open doors and bring down walls,"[12] Governor Ann Richards once said.

Humor, wisdom, and a uniquely Texan brand of populism have helped Richards emerge with style and flourish as one of the decade's most vibrant and energetic leaders.

All of those qualities were embodied in the speech that made her famous—her keynote address at the 1988 Democratic National Convention. Her two-sentence swipe at George Bush made headlines: "Poor George, he can't help it—he was born with a silver foot in his mouth." But what was overlooked was what came just a few moments later: a moving testimonial to America's great leaders. She said she regretted that today's youth missed out on the leaders of earlier decades—"leaders who told us when things were tough and that we'd have to sacrifice, and that these difficulties might last awhile. They didn't tell us things were hard for us because we were different, or isolated, or special interests. They brought us together and they gave us a sense of national purpose."[13]

Texas's first female governor to be elected since 1924—and the state's most celebrated chief since John Connally—has made her mark with plain talk, consensus building, and a passion for diversity.

The only child of a truck driver and homemaker, Richards grew up in a tiny central Texas town. She won a debate scholarship to Baylor University, where she met and married her high school sweetheart. In the mid-1950s, Richards worked for two years teaching junior high school government classes. "Teaching was the hardest work I had ever done," she wrote, "and it remains the hardest work I have done to date."[14]

In 1972, after working on a friend's state legislature campaign, she decided to run herself, and won a seat on the Travis County commission in 1976. Six years later, she ran for Texas treasurer, becoming the first woman in fifty years to hold statewide office.

A lifelong Democrat, she resists simple political labels. She sees the need for government to help the underprivileged, but recognizes the necessity to control its growth. As governor, Richards is a persuasive, strong, and forthright leader. Upon taking office in 1991, she pledged to create a "new Texas," and set to work immediately on an activist agenda, with efforts to tame and streamline the state's sprawling government. The governor quickly imposed a hiring freeze in the state government and filled nearly half of her four hundred appointments to state agencies with members of minority groups. Populist issues have topped her priority list: regulating the insurance industry, enforcing ethics guidelines in government, and reorganizing the bloated state bureaucracy.

She prefers humor to confrontation as a style of consensus building. With her blunt manner and ready wit, Richards has gained acceptance in her native state as a "good ol' girl." A divorced mother of four and a recovering alcoholic, Richards has overcome her share of personal troubles. She spent time in the early eighties in an alcoholic rehabilitation center, and still attends weekly meetings of Alcoholics Anonymous. Though political opponents have tried to use those problems against her, her ability to overcome weaknesses remains, perhaps, one of her strongest attractions for Americans.

THE BLUNT REALIST

WARREN B. RUDMAN
FORMER U.S. SENATOR FROM NEW
  HAMPSHIRE
BORN: MAY 18, 1930,
  BOSTON, MASSACHUSETTS

He has no tolerance for deadlock. He is frank and honest and blunt. He faces the issues head-on.

The same iconoclastic qualities that prompted Sen. Warren Rudman to give up on Capitol Hill would make him a forceful presence on Pennsylvania Avenue.

Rudman was never a popular man in Washington, where he served in the Senate for twelve years (he retired in 1992). He disdained socializing with his congressional colleagues, and he repeatedly turned down invitations to White House dinners. As a senator, he lacked patience for the long-winded debate on the floor of the Senate. He pushed to change the institution's rules to encourage more listening and less needless argument.

Rudman sees the mounting federal deficit as the nation's ultimate issue—one that threatens the very workings of government. He cosponsored the 1985 Gramm-Rudman-Hollings law, the strongest legislative effort to balance the budget. And he has been openly critical of his colleagues' unwillingness to confront the deficit. "We are . . . not watching the fiddler fiddle while Rome burns," he has said. "We are watching the entire orchestra."[15]

Rudman advocated cuts in social programs—and means testing to make sure those benefiting from the services are those most in need—in order to cut federal spending. He consistently claimed that his Senate and House colleagues knew he was right, but were unwilling to risk the political fallout of making such decisions.

"We ought to tell people what the real facts are," he has said. "We ought to do what we have to do, go home and try to defend it."[16]

Rudman was a New Hampshire lawyer in private practice for ten years before serving as the state's attorney general for six years.

His working style is tough and demanding, his manner marked by combativeness, bluntness, and directness. His politics defy easy labels. "The liberals consider me a conservative and the conservatives consider me a liberal," he once said.[17]

A military hawk, he supported the development of the B-1 bomber, opposed the nuclear freeze movement, and encouraged the production of chemical weapons. But on social issues, he opposed efforts to limit abortion and fought the introduction of prayer in public schools.

An iconoclast, he has taken on his own party's leadership—most visibly when he served on the panel investigating the Reagan administration's handling of the Iran-Contra affair.

After leaving the Senate, Rudman returned to private law practice and with former Sen. Paul Tsongas founded the Concord Coalition, a nonpartisan, grassroots group working to break the governmental gridlock and reduce the deficit.

He has said he doesn't wish to return to elective office. Yet his style, candor, and single-mindedness would surely be assets in putting the nation back on course. "Quite frankly," he once said of himself and his congressional colleagues, "we were elected to lead. And we ought to lead."[18]

THE "BOOM-BOOM" MANAGER _____

DONNA SHALALA
U.S. SECRETARY OF HEALTH AND
   HUMAN SERVICES
BORN: FEBRUARY 14, 1941,
   CLEVELAND, OHIO

Donna Shalala abhors bureaucracies; yet she has come to master them. She once feared Washington; yet she adapted and conquered it.

Exuberant, energetic, hardworking, and dynamic, Shalala emerged as one of the nation's top managers in higher education, first as president of Hunter College, the largest campus of the City University of New York, and then as chancellor of the University of Wisconsin. As President Clinton's secretary of health and human services, she heads a department with a $539 billion budget and 125,000 employees.

The first woman to head a Big Ten university, and only the second woman ever to preside over a major U.S. research university, Shalala has gained a reputation as an exceptional executive. Her style is effective and forthright. She sets a vision and achieves it; she delegates power; she retains a sense of compassion and an eye for detail. All of this would stand her in good stead in the Oval Office.

Her friends call her leadership style "boom-boom management." She targets a problem precisely, aims carefully, then attacks it from several angles simultaneously. When she perceived elements of racism and a lack of diversity on the Wisconsin campus, she attacked immediately with a multipart plan to attract low-income students, forge links with minority colleges, and hire more minority faculty members. When she found budget and morale problems in the athletic department, she fired the athletic director and hired in his place an alumnus who was a Rose

Bowl hero and All-American. *BusinessWeek* named her one of the nation's top five managers in higher education.

Shalala was born and raised in Cleveland, Ohio, one of twin daughters of a real-estate salesman and a physical education teacher who later became a lawyer. Shalala has attributed much of her ambition to her mother, a nationally ranked tennis player in her youth who continues to win tournaments in her eighties. In the early 1960s, Shalala spent two years in the Peace Corps, teaching social science in Iran.

Shalala was an academic, an expert on New York City, when she was appointed assistant secretary at the Department of Housing and Urban Development in the Carter administration. She learned to loathe the aggressiveness and bureaucracy of Washington, but she took away lessons. "I learned you have to get a fast start, and you have to have sharp elbows," she said.[19]

While at HUD, Shalala made a specialty of women's issues, establishing special policies to benefit female homeowners, securing financing for battered-women's shelters, and studying the housing needs of families headed by women.

In 1980, at thirty-nine, Shalala became the youngest woman ever to head a college when she took the helm of Hunter. In 1988, she was named chancellor at Wisconsin.

A dynamic leader, Shalala is also a team player. "My secret is hiring people smarter than I am, then delegating,"[20] she has said. She is not one to shy away from touting her own impressive accomplishments—a quality that brings wide attention to the institutions she has led.

THE BOARDROOM PHYSICIAN _____

PINDAROS ROY VAGELOS
PRESIDENT, CHAIRMAN, AND
   CHIEF EXECUTIVE OFFICER,
   MERCK & CO.
BORN: OCTOBER 8, 1929

With foresight, planning, and creativity, Roy Vagelos took a struggling behemoth of a corporation and made it the envy of the pharmaceutical world.

Imagine what he could do for America.

Merck & Co. was an unremarkable giant with a moribund research branch when Vagelos took over in 1976. He directed massive resources to research and development and launched an aggressive effort to recruit the top scientists from the nation's universities. The result: Merck emerged in the eighties to become the undisputed world leader among drug companies, labeled by some business analysts "the best company in the world."[21] *Fortune* magazine named Merck "America's Most Admired Corporation" five years in a row. And in 1990, Vagelos was named Manager of the Year by a coalition of business groups.

Vagelos's success has come about in large part because he possesses that most critical of leadership qualities: vision. He is a long-term planner who made research and development a priority because he knew that it was the key to distinguishing his company from its competitors.

His background as a physician and biochemist makes him one of the few CEOs in his industry with firsthand understanding of the scientific inquiry process. Since 1985, Merck has increased R&D spending at a compound annual rate of 15 percent. In 1992, the company spent more than $1.1 billion on developing new products.[22]

And Vagelos has attracted so many researchers from the nation's top universities that the company's Rahway, New Jersey, headquarters has the feel of a university campus. The results have been impressive: Merck brought ten new drugs to the market in the decade between 1981 and 1991, each netting more than $100 million in annual sales.

Vagelos is willing to bypass normal channels to reward quality work. He is known to promote managers, skipping several rungs on the corporate ladder to maintain a creative and flexible work environment. He is an open-minded manager who keeps his door open to employees.

That informal style stems in part from his background. The tale of his ascent to the boardroom is like something out of Horatio Alger. As a teenager, Vagelos labored in his parents' Rahway Luncheonette—just minutes away from Merck headquarters—where young Roy eavesdropped on company shoptalk and dreamed of a research career.

He worked his way through the University of Pennsylvania and Columbia University's medical school. He was directing biomedical research at Washington University School of Medicine when Merck tapped him to become a top executive.

Vagelos and his company retain a commitment to being good corporate citizens. The Merck Co. Foundation—financed entirely by Merck & Co.—is highly involved in backing educational and community programs. He encourages researchers to work outside the corporate laboratories to help promote cutting-edge research, and he has made a point of supporting education. But that, too, is part of his long-range vision. He wants young people to gain a solid grasp of basic science and math, he says, so the nation will remain competitive in technical fields.[23]

Vagelos's long-range vision, his understanding of the interplay of education and progress, and his creative management style would make him a strong and effective president.

THE VOTE

We mailed ballots—complete with biographical sketches—to a representative sampling of 3,000 Americans. About one-third of those who were approached responded—1,067 people. Ninety-one percent of those participating identified themselves as registered voters. We asked participants in the election to review the résumés and choose one of the candidates—and to write in any desired candidate not on the list.

BUT FIRST, THIS MESSAGE FROM HISTORY

Before we reveal the results of our national referendum on leadership, it's important to consider this question: How reliable is a candidate's track record in determining what sort of president he'd make?

Consider a phenomenon we'll call the Gettysburg Principle.

On November 19, 1863, two men gave speeches at the commemoration of a Pennsylvania military cemetery.

President Abraham Lincoln was an almost universally reviled figure. Many Americans saw him as hopeless, incompetent, a "rube" in way over his head—a man lacking the authority needed during a time of national calamity. His scanty résumé included jobs as a surveyor and a postal clerk, a one-term stint in Congress, and two failed U.S. Senate campaigns.

Edward Everett, on the other hand, had perhaps the most impressive résumé in nineteenth-century America. He'd been a senator, a congressman, a secretary of state, a governor, and a Unitarian minister; and he held two degrees from Harvard.

In fact, most of the six thousand people attending the commemoration came to hear Everett, reputed to be the nation's greatest orator. The event's planners invited Lincoln only as a begrudging afterthought.

That day at Gettysburg, Edward Everett spoke for exactly one hour and fifty-seven minutes.

And no one remembers a word he uttered.

Lincoln spoke for two minutes.

And the nation will forever remember every word.

The lesson: Leadership is sometimes unpredictable.

We launched our search for presidential candidates, armed with the caveat that leadership ability may well arise from the most unlikely of sources:

- *Woodrow Wilson* was an academic who first ran for political office three years before he became president.
- *Harry Truman* had only a high school education.

In sum, it's worth keeping in mind that those with the best potential for leadership don't always look the best on paper. Sometimes a leader is just a leader.

☆

The American electoral process doesn't select the best leaders. It chooses the best campaigners. The problem with our presidential campaigns is that they have become rigorous, exhausting tests—of the wrong traits. They focus on debating skill, not clarity of vision; they find candidates who can manage photo opportunities, not bureaucracies.

The result: voters have been left cold, trudging off to the polls to choose the least offensive candidate. That's why we chose not to emulate the two-party process. Instead, we concocted the best possible way to answer three basic questions:

- What do Americans want in a president?
- Who are the people who best meet those criteria?
- Of these, which is the best leader?

We conducted no campaign, no debates, no conventions. Our voters simply chose the best leaders. Ours wasn't a referendum on image, it was an assessment of the ability to lead.

We didn't set out to find the best *politician*—nor did we exclude politicians. We took away all the artificial limitations and manipulations of campaigns. We let the people speak.

And speak they did.

Before we move on to the results, it's worth keeping in mind some of the most prominent political axioms of 1990s America. These are the trends pundits throw around with such frequency that they've become clichés:

- Americans don't want professional politicians as their leaders anymore.
- Supply-side economics is dead.

58

- The Republicans have had their chance.
- Americans are thirsting for women in leadership positions.

Here's what our "election" told us about those sentiments: they're all *dead wrong.*

THE FINAL TALLY

When we counted the votes, the winner was clear:

Rank	Candidate	Percent of Vote
1	Jack Kemp	27.2 percent
2	John Bryan	16.4 percent
3	Ann Richards	14.5 percent
4	Warren Rudman	12.5 percent
5	Donna Shalala	10.3 percent
6	Roy Vagelos	6.8 percent
7	Barbara Jordan	6.5 percent

MEANING IN THE NUMBERS

The results say as much about the voters as about the candidates. The enthusiastic support for Ross Perot's 1992 candidacy made it clear: Americans are as fed up with the electoral *process* as they are with the politicians themselves. They're seeking solutions to the nation's leadership vacuum by looking beyond the traditional venues.

So it's no mistake that Jack Kemp, the runaway winner, is an iconoclastic figure who has achieved a national stature but who doesn't fit neatly into either major party. As much as his economic approach clearly reflects Republican, conservative doctrine, his social outlook puts him more in line with many Democrats. Kemp hasn't found success as a candidate in the party system, but in our nonpartisan race, he cleaned up.

Our conclusion: The present system doesn't succeed at reflecting the will of the people, only the will of the parties.

WHO SUPPORTS KEMP?

Jack Kemp is known as a neoconservative, yet he had appeal to voters of all outlooks:

No surprise. Kemp naturally won the race among those who identify themselves as his ideological allies:

- Conservatives: 40 percent
- Republicans: 57 percent
- Those with household incomes over $50,000: 26 percent

Crossing over. But Kemp also found backers from a surprising array of groups. In a wide range of categories, he was the top pick:

- Hispanics: 37 percent
- Unskilled blue-collar workers: 31 percent
- Those with household incomes under $30,000: 30 percent
- Moderates: 27 percent
- Women: 23 percent

Falling short. Kemp had his poorest showing among those groups most clearly outside his camp.

- *Clintonians.* Kemp placed fourth among those who voted for President Clinton in 1992—with just one in ten votes.
- *Liberals.* He was fourth among liberals, with 11 percent.
- *Democrats.* He took fourth place among Democrats, with just 9 percent.

THE NAME GAME

Was Jack Kemp just a familiar face? Was name recognition the only factor in the voter's choice? Clearly, familiarity had some impact—but it was marginal. How do we know? Because of our second-place winner: John Bryan, a virtual unknown to most Americans. Bryan beat out a nationally known governor, a revered senator, even a current Cabinet member. This wasn't a popularity contest.

A SLEEPER IN SECOND _____

It's clear: Americans are eager for leaders from outside the realm of traditional politics. In 1992, it was Ross Perot. In our election, that yearning took the form of enthusiastic backing for John Bryan. Nearly every subgroup of voters made Bryan their second choice. Certainly, voters were impressed with Bryan's leadership strengths and his managerial skills. And his high ranking helped prove our assumption: Many Americans are fed up with the same old names. They want leaders.

Choice of the disaffected. In fact, those who identify least with traditional political parties and labels were most likely to opt for Bryan.

- *Independents.* Bryan won among independents, nabbing 25 percent of the vote—compared to Kemp's 20 percent.
- *Moderates.* Bryan finished a close second, with 20 percent, compared to Kemp's 25 percent.
- *Retired people.* Bryan was the top vote getter among retired people, with 25 percent.

Votes from all over. Bryan found support among a wide variety of voter groups.

- *Democrats and liberals.* Bryan was second to Ann Richards in both categories, with 18 percent and 16 percent.
- *Broad appeal.* Bryan placed second in the vast majority of groups:

  - Men: 18 percent
  - Married Americans: 18 percent
  - Employed: 17 percent
  - Unemployed: 16 percent
  - Baby boomers (30–49): 18 percent
  - Younger voters (18–29): 23 percent

THE FAITHFUL LEFT _____

Old loyalties die hard. Those who traditionally support Democratic presidential nominees placed themselves behind one in this race. Ann Richards, the liberal Democratic Texas governor, was the clear winner among Democrats with 27 percent, and liberals (31 percent).

THE FEMININE MYSTIQUE

Is America ready to elect a woman president? Maybe not. Even though three of our seven finalists were women, the group didn't fare well. Our voters didn't overwhelmingly choose to vote for people of their own gender, but obviously, gender made a difference. Jack Kemp was the clear leader among women, with 23 percent—though Ann Richards placed second among women with 17 percent.

Still, it was striking how large a portion of support for women candidates came from women voters.

- *The female factor.* What percentage of each candidate's votes came from women?
  - Ann Richards: 66 percent
  - Donna Shalala: 80 percent
  - Barbara Jordan: 87 percent

IF IT'S AN ELECTION, THIS MUST BE . . . PEROT

The other big question about presidential politics in the nineties is: Can you keep Perot out of the picture?

The answer: Maybe not.

Though we excluded Ross Perot—the Texas billionaire and '92 presidential candidate—from our ballot, he found his way on. When we asked for write-in candidates, *10 percent* of all voters listed Perot.

A REFERENDUM ON LEADERSHIP

It would be easy to read our results as a referendum on supply-side economics. Or a shift in party loyalties. But that would also be simplistic. We see something deeper: we read the results as a statement about leadership.

Remember the "Seven C's"—the qualities Americans wanted in their leaders? Character, competence, commitment, confidence, clarity, compassion, charisma. Those are the qualities that came to the surface in this election. It's clear that those are the qualities Americans yearn for in their leaders. Perot's wide appeal in 1992 shows that the American people are trying to reclaim some political leverage from the parties and their process. Americans have made their statement: They've had it with party politics, with having decisions made for them, with identical, sound-bite candidates. Americans are yearning for a way to let their true choices rise to the top.

★

I I	
# SOLVE-AT-ALL-COSTS ISSUES	
A THE ECONOMY	
B EDUCATION	
C HEALTH CARE	
D CRIME	
E DRUGS	

★

Some problems can wait—until tomorrow, until next month, maybe until a few years from now.

But some can't wait another minute.

This section is about the ones that can't wait.

The issues we'll discuss in this section are challenges that threaten the very survival of the nation. Everyone agrees on that—conservatives, liberals, the rich, the poor, people of all ethnic groups. Everyone. These aren't theoretical matters to be debated in obscure journals. These are questions that spell life and death for America—the issues we must solve at all costs.

These topics aren't on the sidelines. They're at the center of attention. If we don't find solutions to these issues—and soon—the United States could well plunge into indigence. If we keep putting off these concerns, we risk falling to the status of a third-world country.

Why haven't we solved these issues yet? We discovered that many of the debates have focused on the wrong issues, and ignored some of the most valid solutions. By listening to the people, we came up with solutions that have been over-looked—but creative, valid options that offer hope for the nation.

THE ISSUES

The issues Americans ranked at the top of their lists are matters that the government continues to grapple with, to little effect. They're the issues we keep hearing about on the news—because they just won't go away. But they must.

- *The Economy.* Once the pride of the world, the American economy has lost ground to Japan, Germany, and other industrialized nations. Americans found a way to save the national economy from the brink of disaster.

67

- *Education.* Literacy rates are plunging. Our children can't read maps or do math. Yet education holds the key to any hope for future prosperity. Americans came up with alternatives to upgrade our schools and meet the challenge.
- *Health Care.* Since the 1992 election, health care has been a hot topic. Yet 37 million Americans still lack health insurance, and the debate has merely muddied the waters. Americans had surprising ideas for solving the health-care quagmire.
- *Crime.* Violence is ripping apart the very fabric of our cities and towns. Millions of Americans live in constant fear of crime. Americans concocted innovative approaches to curbing crime.
- *Drugs.* The decade-long war on drugs has had little impact, as illegal drugs continue to damage families, neighborhoods, workplaces—and to destroy lives. Americans made it clear how the nation can win the battle.

THE TIME IS NOW

The beauty of American democracy is that everyone's ideas count. The forum is always open. But on these issues, it's time to stop debating. It's time to act. Before it's too late.

THE ECONOMY

The streets were paved with gold.

That was the image that captured the hearts of the hundreds of thousands of immigrants who flooded America's shores earlier in this century: a nation of unbridled prosperity, of growth, of endless opportunity.

And now? Latter-day newcomers to America's decaying cities are lucky if they find the streets paved at all.

The past decade has thrust the nation into an economic tailspin. After decades of constant growth, America's financial machine slowed down to a crawl.

- Workers' salaries plunged.
- Unemployment soared.
- Japanese and Western European nations came to dominate industries formerly controlled by American companies.

Is it time to give up hope?

We don't think so.

We're going to fix the economy. Starting right now. We knew the ideas were out there—they just weren't being put to work. The key to solving our economic ills is to stop talking about them, and *take action*.

When we looked for solutions, we found them. And we took them to the people. Intellectuals try to make economics complicated and inaccessible. We learned that the American people have a keen grasp of what makes the economy tick. When we listened, we found that they had the questions—and the answers. The people are tired of inaction. They're ready to move with resolve. So they led us to the answers.

First we'll draw some lessons from the mistakes of the past. And then we'll get to work fixing the economy. Not tomorrow.

Now.

BOOM, BOOM, BUST

It's easiest to comprehend the sorry state of America's economy if you look at how far we've fallen.

A snapshot of the burgeoning U.S. economy of 1950s America:

- The American market was more than nine times bigger than the next largest, the United Kingdom.[1]
- The United States created 59 percent of the world's total industrial output.[2]
- The United States accounted for half the world's gross national product.[3]
- America's GNP per capita was twice Canada's; three times the United Kingdom's; four times West Germany's; and fifteen times Japan's.[4]

DECADES ON THE RISE

That success wasn't a short-lived fluke of history.

The secret to America's affluence has been our unrivaled history of consistent economic growth.

The American economy averaged a yearly growth rate of about 3 percent for 150 years—between the 1820s and the 1970s.[5] That means the living standard doubled every twenty-one years.[6]

For most of American history, the average American living to age sixty-five saw the standard of living quadruple!

At the current rate, it would take more than fifty-eight years—an American's entire career—to see a doubling of living standards.[7]

The past decade's plunge has shattered that record of growth.

WE'RE NOT NUMBER ONE

Who has the world's largest integrated economy? The European Community. Its GNP in 1990 was nearly *$7 trillion*, compared to $5.5 trillion for the United States and nearly $3 trillion for Japan.[8]

In fact, while America's economy was fifteen times larger than Japan's GNP four decades ago—that is, *1,500 percent* larger—in 1990, it was just *40 percent* larger (though America's population is twice Japan's).[9]

FACE THE FACTS

The shabby state of the American economy isn't a partisan issue. It's not a matter of opinion. The numbers speak for themselves. It's simply not debatable: the economy has toppled; America, Inc., is losing its market share.

Industry can't compete. The main reason for the economy's rapid tumble: U.S. businesses just don't stack up.

Sagging corporate power. In 1970, sixty-four of the world's top one hundred corporations were American. In 1988? Just forty-two!

Tumbling profits. American manufacturing corporations have seen shrinking profits since the mid-1960s—tumbling from a peak of 12.7 percent (after taxes) in the sixties, to 10 percent in the mid-seventies, to less than 7 percent in the eighties.[10]

Manufacturing in decline. The proportion of America's manufacturing capacity being used in production has been falling since the mid-sixties. Manufacturing capacity was employed at 86 percent of capacity in 1965, 80 percent in the seventies, and below 70 percent in the eighties.[11]

Slipping market share. In several key categories, America's dominance has fallen sharply. Since 1963, America's proportions of world sales have plunged in key areas:[12]

- Autos: down nearly one-third
- Industrial machinery: down one-third
- Agricultural machinery: down 40 percent
- Telecommunications machinery: down 50 percent

Trade imbalance. A look at the top six products traded between Japan and the United States makes America look like a backward banana republic:

WHAT WE SELL THE JAPANESE _____

1. Corn seed
2. Soybeans
3. Coal
4. Wood
5. Cotton
6. Wheat[13]

WHAT THE JAPANESE SELL US _____

1. Automobiles
2. Tape recorders
3. Trucks
4. Office machines
5. Parts for office machines
6. Computer chips[14]

Ailing banks. In service industries, too, American business has tumbled from its dominance.

- Nine of the world's top ten service corporations are Japanese.[15]
- The number of American banks in the world's top fifty fell from nineteen in 1970 to five in 1988.[16] (By 1990, *no* American bank was in the world's top twenty.)[17]

PRODUCTIVITY PLUNGES

Americans' standard of living may soon *drop* for the first time in history.

In 1989 and 1990, America's productivity—the amount produced per worker per hour—actually declined.[18]

And the crisis dates back three decades: since the mid-1960s, America's economic growth has paled compared to the growth of Japan, West Germany, France, Italy, and Great Britain.[19]

REALITY HITS HOME

American workers are earning less money.

The worsening economic slump isn't just a numbers game. It translates into a stark reality: the shattering of the American dream.

American parents have always been certain their children would be better off than they were—as long as they worked hard.

No more. That hope is all but dead.

Shrinking paychecks. The drop in productivity means American workers take home less money.

- In 1990, American earning power (per person GNP)—once the world's highest—had slipped behind Switzerland, Iceland, Japan, Norway, Sweden, Finland, Denmark, and Germany.[20]

Stagnant income. American workers are finding that their pay isn't going up.

- Median real family incomes in 1990 stayed at 1973 levels.[21]
- In 1991, the real purchasing power of the typical American family shrank by $1,000—the second straight year household income declined.[22]

THE MIDDLE-CLASS CRUNCH

America's middle class is shrinking.

American salaries are falling. That means, for the first time, America is facing the prospect of ceasing to be a middle-class society.

What percentages of other populations are middle-class?[23]

- Japan: 90 percent
- Sweden: 79 percent
- Norway: 73 percent
- Germany: 70 percent

And America's?

- 54 percent

TYCOONS AND PAUPERS

As the rich get richer, the poor get poorer.

As the nation's economy plunged in the 1980s, a disturbing trend emerged: America became a nation of haves and have-nots—of the very needy and the very rich.

The millionaire index. Oddly, the number of people earning extremely high incomes bears little relation to the overall state of the economy:

- During the economic boom of the 1950s, the number of Americans with annual incomes of $500,000 or more rose from 842 to 1,002— a *19 percent* surge.[24]
- During the 1980s, as the national debt mounted and the growth rate shrank, the number soared from 16,881 in 1980 to 183,240 in 1989—a *985 percent* spurt.[25]

The indigence index. At the same time, those with the least became needier.

- The percentage of U.S. wealth controlled by the poorest fifth of the population shrank from 5.5 percent in 1970 to 3.7 percent in 1990.
- From 1977 to 1990, the average incomes of the poorest fifth of American families fell by *7 percent* (while the richest fifth increased 15 percent).[26]
- A staggering 35.7 million Americans are now below the poverty level—the highest number since before the 1964 War on Poverty.

Unprecedented extremes. Indeed, by 1990, the wealthiest fifth of the population had the highest proportion of income ever recorded for the group, and the bottom three-fifths the least.[27]

Strained by taxes. To make matters worse, the wealthiest Americans got tax breaks, while the poorest were burdened with *higher taxes.*[28]

WORKING FOR PEANUTS

More and more, working Americans are earning less and less.

The persistent myth is that America's poor are an indigent, unemployable underclass. In reality, the lower echelons of American society have come to be occupied by a growing class: the working poor.

- Today, more than half the 32.5 million Americans below the poverty line come from working households.[29]
- Nearly two-thirds of all poor children live in households with at least one employed worker.[30]

The sharp increase in the working poor stemmed in part from a massive shift in American industry: During the eighties, industry cut hundreds of thousands of manufacturing jobs. At the same time, there was a sharp rise in low-paying service-sector jobs: hamburger cooks, hospital orderlies, messengers. Since 1973, the increase in employment in eating and drinking places alone has been greater than the total employment in America's auto and steel industries combined.[31]

NO JOBS

Pink slips are becoming commonplace.

Because the United States has failed to train its workers to adapt to changes in the economic scene, its jobless rate has reached a higher plateau than ever before. In the late 1960s, unemployment averaged about 3.5 percent.[32] But since the mid-1980s, the rate has hovered between 7 and 8 percent.

NO TRAINING

Why has unemployment remained high? Because the nation has not trained its workforce. America has *no mechanism* in place to save its workers from unemployment and dead-end jobs and bring them into the kinds of industries where Americans can gain and maintain a competitive advantage while preserving or increasing their real wages.[33]

THE ECHOES OF UNEMPLOYMENT

And unemployment is a curse that reverberates through the economy. Every 1 percent increase in the jobless rate costs roughly

- $75 billion in lost production of goods and services
- $25 billion in lost taxes
- $5 billion in unemployment compensation

The nation's neglect of job training has created a core of unskilled workers, virtually guaranteeing decades of high unemployment.

WHAT RUINED US: THE FOUR FAILURES

Why has the American economy declined? We've neglected:

- the eroding infrastructure
- research and development
- worker training
- the mounting deficit

CRUMBLING AT THE CORE

The nation's infrastructure is eroding.

America has neglected its physical infrastructure—its highways and bridges, as well as its manufacturing facilities. Meanwhile its competitors have allotted massive resources to build theirs up.

Insufficient investment. In the 1950s and '60s, the nation's businesses constantly increased their investment in plants and equipment. But in the 1970s and '80s, they neglected capital investment.[34]

Trailing the competition. The Japanese and Germans have poured their wealth into upgrading the physical infrastructure necessary to succeed in the competitive world economy. The United States simply hasn't.

BAD SCIENCE

America is neglecting research and development.

America prides itself on innovation. The Model T, the phonograph, the polio vaccine—all came from American ingenuity.

Neglecting innovation. But we've forgotten the importance of new ideas and breakthroughs.

- The United States ranks twentieth out of twenty-three industrialized countries in private spending on research and development.[35]
- The American Council on Competitiveness assessed the nation's technological position and gave the United States a grade of B-minus.[36]

A drop in patents. For proof of America's lagging ingenuity, look at the drop in inventions. How many of the top ten U.S. patent winners were American corporations?

- In 1970: seven
- In 1990: three[37]

Fewer advanced degrees. Why aren't we making the technological breakthroughs we once did? Perhaps it's because we simply don't have the innovators anymore.

- America now produces fewer than half the Ph.D. engineers and scientists per capita that it did in the early 1970s.[38]

AN OBSOLETE WORKFORCE

The nation has simply overlooked the importance of training workers.

America once prided itself on an education system that was second to none, and on an enlightened, proud labor force. As we've rested on our laurels, the world has passed us by.

Ailing schools. We're giving our kids a mathematical education that puts them in sorry shape against their counterparts elsewhere.

- The math scores of the top 1 percent of American high school seniors would place them behind *one-half* their counterparts in Japan.[39]

Poor worker training. When compared to the extensive training for workers in other leading industrial countries, America's worker training is an embarrassment.

While other nations have made training for workers an integral part of society, America has virtually ignored the idea. As a result, workers in other countries can rapidly adapt to new industries and technologies. And Americans? We simply lose our jobs.

At any given time, what percentage of workers are training for new jobs?

- In Germany, Japan, Sweden, and France: between *1 and 2 percent.*
- In the United States: *one-tenth of 1 percent.*[40]

The German advantage. Germany gives every adult up to two years of full-time training or retraining. More than half of the program's participants are employed people who want to improve their skills. (The government pays all training costs and provides an income subsidy.)[41]

Japan's approach. Japan provides unemployed workers in designated "structurally depressed industries" with generous job-training and placement assistance, linked to unemployment benefits.[42]

DIGGING OUR OWN GRAVE

Three factors are devastating the economy:

- The trade deficit
- Mounting debt
- Low savings

LOSING THE GLOBAL MARKET

As American industry has become more tied to international trade, the nation has seen an increasing imbalance in business with its competitors.

Foreign dominance. Since the mid-1960s, imports have bombarded the U.S. market. By 1981 the United States was importing[43]

- 26 percent of its cars
- 25 percent of its steel
- 60 percent of its TVs, radios, tape recorders, and stereos
- 43 percent of its calculators

Twenty years before, imports had accounted for *less than 10 percent* of each category.

Falling behind. During the 1970s, the share of American-made goods in total world sales dropped by 23 percent, while *every other industrialized nation except Great Britain* maintained or expanded its share.[44]

Growing deficits. Since 1984, the United States has averaged overall trade deficits of around $100 billion annually.[45] In 1989, the deficit was $130 billion (2.3 percent of the national income).

SHRINKING SAVINGS

Americans—even in hard times—remain disturbingly avid consumers. Even though the economy has stopped growing, Americans have continued their high level of consumption by borrowing more and saving less.

- Americans are the most indebted people on earth, with household debt averaging $71,500, *twice* that of Great Britain, and *eighty-nine times* that of Switzerland.[46]
- America's savings per household is $4,201—less than *one-third* that of Germany, and less than *one-tenth* that of Japan.

THE CURSE OF THE DEFICIT

Following the lead of its citizens, the federal government continues to build up a debt of its own.

- By the mid-1980s, the federal deficit for one year exceeded the gross national product of 167 countries.[47]
- The U.S. budget deficit equals the combined trade surpluses of the European Community, Japan, Taiwan, and Korea.[48]

FIXING THE ECONOMIC MESS: THE PHILOSOPHICAL CHOICES

How to repair the economy? There are as many plans as there are economists. But the myriad approaches tend to cluster around a few distinct central concepts.

THE BASIC UNIT: ME OR US?

Some approaches to economic life revolve around the contributions and benefits of the *individual*, while others focus on aiding the *collective*.

The individual. The first approach assumes that the ultimate motivation for all human economic activity is self-interest. In this view, the economy's prime mover is the individual: the worker, the consumer, the entrepreneur. And the best economic system provides incentives for individuals to work hard, to invest, to innovate, and to produce more.

The individual approach abhors state regulation, arguing that government interference works to stifle the economy. Rather, abstract market principles and human incentives ought to be the factors guiding economic activity.

The collective. The second approach views economic activity as an essentially social endeavor, conducted for the mutual benefit of all participants. In this approach, success depends on cooperation—not antagonism—among business, labor, and government.

THE PRIORITY: THE GLOBE OR THE NATION? ___

Some approaches emphasize world perspective; others stress the prominence of competing nations.

Globalism. As multinational corporations multiply, this view holds, the world is becoming one large free market. Nationality is fading in importance, and companies must work to succeed without regard for national borders.

Nationalism. This economic worldview recognizes that in the wake of the Cold War, economic conflict has replaced military and ideological conflict. Military alliances may be fading in importance, but international trading blocs are gaining prominence.

CHOOSING A PATH: FOUR OPTIONS FOR ECONOMIC DIRECTION

Merging these views in various combinations, we came up with four general approaches. Each plan is unique in perspective. The questions arise:

- How strong a role should the government have in repairing the economy?
- What is the impact of the world outside the United States?
- Should the United States be cooperative or cutthroat in the cauldron of the international economy?

THE COMMUNITARIAN-NATIONALIST MODEL ___

This plan—championed by Lester Thurow, dean of the Sloan School of Business Management at MIT—calls for two significant shifts in approach:

- *Federal role.* Give the government an increasingly active role in overhauling the economy.
- *Managed trade.* Create a managed trade policy that plays by the same rules as America's successful competitors.

Domestic cooperation. The idea: Our free-market model can't compete with other countries' policies, which encourage collaboration among business, government, labor, and management.

Currently, U.S. policy gives government no role in funding and strategically coordinating industry. Business leaders view government as incompetent, bureaucratic, and inefficient. And our antitrust laws pit sectors against each other, outlawing collusion.

But burgeoning nations like Japan and Germany have thrived precisely because government and business work hand in hand.

- *Government ownership.* In Germany, the government owns more shares in industries—from airlines to automakers—than in any non-Communist country in the world.
- *State leadership.* In Japan, representatives of the powerful Ministry of International Trade develop strategic visions for the economy and direct research money into emerging industries.

International competition. This approach further claims that America has significantly lost ground in the world by sticking with a free-market approach to global trade. We've slipped behind nations that make profits from American consumers but freeze U.S. companies out of their own markets.

THE COMMUNITARIAN-GLOBALIST MODEL ⎯⎯⎯⎯

This approach, long backed by Secretary of Labor Robert B. Reich, starts with these assumptions about today's world economy:

- National lines mean nothing.
- Wealth is determined by infrastructure, education, and worker skills.
- Traditional production modes are giving way to flexible systems.

"The ubiquitous and irrepressible law of supply and demand no longer respects national borders," Reich has written. There will be "no such thing as an American corporation or an American industry. The American economy is but a region of the global economy."[49]

In the modern global marketplace, money moves around easily. Strength comes from immobile factors—like skills and physical facilities.

In that view, three priorities are vital to making the United States competitive. The nation must

- Invest in infrastructure
- Invest in education
- Invest in training workers

In Reich's view, American manufacturing is too structured and too inflexible to adapt to changing technology. Our industries, geared for the *mass production* of the past, should reshape themselves for the *niche production* of the future. We have specialized machines; we need flexible ones. We have unskilled workers; we need skilled ones.

"Industries of the future will not depend on physical 'hardware,' which can be duplicated anywhere, but on the human 'software,' which can reattain a technological edge," Reich has written.[50]

With that in mind, this approach calls on government to help industry adapt to the production processes of the future. Government would provide aid—not with tax breaks or tariffs, but by giving aid to businesses that restructure and invest in training.

THE INDIVIDUALISTIC-NATIONALIST MODEL

The approach of the Council on Competitiveness views the individual as central to the U.S. economy and society, but backs some coordination among labor, business, and government.

The objective:

- To help the United States compete in the world market

The means:

- To promote cooperation within the private sector
- To urge the government to negotiate trade pacts and enforce fair practices in the global market

The approach rejects sweeping, rapid policy shifts. It advocates gradual, incremental changes in business, labor, academia, and government. It argues that business should work with government to create farsighted policies to help America compete in the world.

THE INDIVIDUALISTIC-GLOBALIST MODEL

Supply-side economics—the view held by Jack Kemp, President Bush's secretary of housing and urban development—makes a basic assumption about human behavior:

- People will work hard, innovate, save, and invest when they're rewarded for these activities. When they're not rewarded, they won't.

In this view, the goal of any economic approach is to increase incentives for productive behavior—for both individuals and nations.

The plan calls for three basic measures to stimulate the economy:

- Cut taxes
- Stabilize the dollar
- Reduce government regulation

Cut taxes. This approach holds that lower taxes mean workers keep more of what they earn—so they have impetus to work harder, produce more, and invest more.

Doesn't that mean less money for the government? No. Supply-siders argue that the larger economy raises the same amount of revenue—but from growth, not high taxes.

Stabilize the dollar. This strategy says inflation results from an oversupply of money. So the government should solve this problem by fixing global exchange rates—by returning to the gold standard.

Reduce regulation. The primary goal of Kemp's strategy is to encourage entrepreneurs to start businesses, to invest, and to hire people. Cutting government interference, he argues, encourages entrepreneurs to base their actions on economic common sense—not pressure from external restrictions.

SOLVING THE ECONOMIC CRISIS: FOUR OPTIONS

SOLUTION NO. 1: THE THUROW PLAN _____

Taxes. Revamp the tax system to enforce strong incentives to save and consume.

- Raise down payments for consumer loans and mortgages (to encourage saving and discourage overconsuming).
- Impose value-added taxes (to promote exports, not domestic consumption).
- Make savings accounts tax-free—but impose taxes on consumption.

Investment. Create strong incentives for private investment and more federal money for public investment.

- Eliminate payroll taxes (to encourage investment in human resources).
- Abolish corporate income taxes (to stimulate investment in infrastructure).

Education. Enhance education and worker training.

- Upgrade public education to make us competitive with our European and Asian counterparts.
- Develop a post–high school track for the non-college-bound.
- Require corporations to *provide* worker training or *pay* into public worker-training funds.
- Expand social security to include training for the young (they'd pay back through payroll deductions).

Cooperation. Let American businesses form coalitions to compete with their foreign equivalents.

- Permit financial institutions to become merchant banks (to own—or be owned by—industrial corporations).

- Allow for the creation of vertical business groups (e.g., financial, automotive, automotive parts suppliers in collaboration).

Countermeasures. Fight policies enacted by other nations by matching competitors dollar for dollar, regulation for regulation, subsidy for subsidy.

- If foreign industrial policies hinder American industries, fight back with countermeasures.
- Practice "targeted" protectionism—precisely focusing on crucial growth industries.
- Encourage government investment and cooperation in spurring research and development in growth industries.

SOLUTION NO. 2: THE REICH PLAN

Training. Move to improve America's workforce.

- Step up job training with a voucher system for on-the-job education (financed by taxing both employers and workers).
- Use tax incentives to encourage companies to invest in improving employees' skills.

Infrastructure. Move to spur investment in the infrastructure.

- Allow tax deductions on interest paid only on loans used to purchase new assets or modernize old ones.
- Set up regional banks to provide low-interest, long-term loans to industries that overhaul themselves to become more competitive.

No layoffs. Remove incentives for businesses to balance their books by firing employees.
Taxes. Encourage savings by not taxing personal income as long as it remains in savings—but taxing money spent on consumption.
Strategy. Establish a public board to oversee government-

business programs to coordinate the nation's long-term economic strategy.

SOLUTION NO. 3: THE COUNCIL ON COMPETITIVENESS PLAN _____

Fiscal reform. Reform the nation's fiscal policy.

- Implement a plan to reduce the deficit.
- Enforce four-year spending caps for entitlement programs, defense, and "mandatory" spending.
- Promote investments in human resources, public infrastructure, and science and technology.
- Create ways to promote private savings, including tax-code changes.

R&D. Promote research and development.

- Appoint a Cabinet-level science and technology czar.
- Pump money into government programs that help derive commercial benefits from technology.
- Encourage laws and regulations that help bring technology to commerce.
- Increase government investment in the nation's technology infrastructure: education, facilities, and equipment.
- Encourage cooperation in research and development, the introduction of new technology into the marketplace, and the creation of a strong industrial base.
- Make research and development tax provisions consistent over the long term (and make the R&D tax credit permanent).

Trade. Reform our approach to global trade.

- Develop mechanisms to coordinate presidential and congressional action on trade issues.
- Pursue trade pacts with Japan and Europe to ensure U.S. access to these important markets.

- Continue efforts to strengthen the General Agreement on Tariffs and Trade (GATT).
- Work to stabilize the dollar.

Training. Invest in training workers for the emerging high-tech, global economy.

- Restructure the elementary and secondary school systems.
- Expand programs serving the disadvantaged.
- Develop and implement federal training programs for workers with outdated skills.
- Revamp labor laws to make them relevant to today's cutthroat global environment.

SOLUTION NO. 4: THE KEMP SUPPLY-SIDE PLAN _

Taxes. Cut taxes.

- Cut income-tax rates across the board.
- Phase in an increase in the personal exemption—which hasn't kept pace with inflation—to relieve families' tax burdens.
- Reduce the capital gains tax—to a maximum of 15 percent and to zero for long-term investments.
- Index the capital gains tax to stop taxing "illusory" gains caused by inflation.
- Allow businesses to recover the full present value of their investment in new equipment.
- Require a three-fifths majority of Congress to raise taxes.

Currency. Stabilize the dollar.

- Control inflation and interest rates by requiring the Federal Reserve to follow price level targeting.
- Call for a global summit to stabilize the world monetary system and streamline tariff policies.

Deregulation. Reduce government regulation.

- Shrink and revamp government to spur investment and growth.
- Make state-run businesses private, sell their assets, and contract out their services.

Spending. Control federal spending.

- Freeze domestic spending.
- Severely cut defense spending.
- Cap spending on entitlement programs—except to account for inflation and population growth.

The poor. Attack poverty.

- Create "free enterprise zones"—and eliminate all capital gains taxes for those who work, save, or invest in them.
- Provide incentives for the poor to work rather than collect welfare, and remove tax incentives for families to choose welfare over work.

The world. Support democratic capitalism around the world, and extend the benefits of free trade.

- Complete the Uruguay round of the General Agreement on Tariffs and Trade (GATT).
- Complete the North American Free Trade Agreement with Mexico and Canada.

THE PEOPLE SPEAK... ☆ ☆

ON THE ECONOMY

MYTHMAKING, MYTHBREAKING

The messages of the contemporary economic gurus are clear:

- We've got to develop our economic infrastructure.
- We must foster competitiveness.
- Our hope lies in promoting economic nationalism.
- Supply-side economics is a failure.

Americans' response is even clearer:

- Wrong.
- Wrong.
- Wrong.
- Dead wrong.

SUPPLY-SIDE LANDSLIDE

When Americans got the chance to consider four widely divergent plans to fix our ailing economy, a huge number of them favored returning to the strategy advocated for twelve years by the Reagan and Bush administrations.

How many Americans support a return to supply-side? Fifty-six percent.

SUPPORT FROM EVERY CORNER

Who supports supply-side? Nearly everyone!
The right.

- Republicans: 60 percent
- Conservatives: 69 percent

The left.

- Democrats: 57 percent

The center.

- Independents: 46 percent
- Moderates: 60 percent

The young.

- Ages 18–29: 88 percent

The poor.

- Income under $30,000: 54 percent

Minorities.

- Blacks and Hispanics: over 75 percent

LIBERAL DISSENT

Only self-defined liberals rejected the supply-side solution to the economy. Among liberals, the results were:

- Supply-side: 24 percent
- The Reich Plan: 43 percent

THE VALUE OF WORK

What happened? The results lead to some obvious questions: Wasn't Bill Clinton's victory over George Bush in 1992 a clear rejection of twelve years of supply-side economic strategy? Hasn't the nation rejected supply-side as a scam perpetrated by greedy conservatives?

Clearly, the answer to each question is: No.

Obviously, Americans were ready to dump the Republican administration. But apparently it wasn't their economic plan that was the problem.

Why do so many Americans support supply-side? The answer isn't greed. It's something inherent in the American character: Americans value hard work and independence. In the midst of our nation's growing problems, most Americans simply don't trust the government and its bureaucracies to solve problems. That message is clear in the economic choices Americans made. It's also clear in their leadership choice—the overwhelming support for Jack Kemp, the biggest backer of supply-side. For all the talk in 1992 about the end of Reaganomics, there might have been a hidden message: It's not that Americans rejected the economic plan; it's that it wasn't carried out.

There's another message: The economic solution isn't the American government. It's the American *people*. And the supply-side plan is the one that leaves the least to the government and gives the most credence to the will and power of individuals.

EDUCATION

We've cleaned up the schools.

We've brought in better teachers.

We've found ways to guarantee that no matter where you happen to live in America—Beverly Hills, or Omaha, or the South Bronx—there's a good, safe school in the neighborhood for your kids.

We've made the public schools serve the public.

How? The people found ways—they're all in this chapter.

Here's the idea we started with: Everything depends on education. Nothing in this book can be accomplished without an educated population. Not safer cities. Not better health care. Not a thriving economy.

Nothing.

Americans know that. They told us it's a top priority to fix the way we teach our children. So we asked them to figure out how to do that. And they came through.

This country achieved greatness by educating the masses. Americans conceived the very idea of public education. We were the first nation to require school from first to the eighth grade—and the first to create a system of mass higher education.

So what went wrong?

Look at the paradox:

- *The top:* In the last four decades, America produced more than three times more Nobel Prize winners in the sciences than any other country.[1]
- *The bottom:* Thirteen percent of American kids leave school with no reading skills whatsoever—more than in any other industrial nation.[2]

Simply put, American education no longer serves the people; it serves the elite.

We've corrected that. By the end of this chapter, you'll see that we've found the big fix for education. We've found ways to make sure America's young people can read and write and learn to grapple with new technology.

Here's how we did it: We didn't get our answers from the people who are in the midst of the problems. We didn't seek advice from the principals, the teachers, or the school-board members, whose districts are struggling to educate children year after year—with declining rates of success. We got help from the people who had the most to say—not because they have professional expertise or advanced degrees, but because they've paid attention to what's happened to the schools. They're the parents and the employers, the regular citizens who see what poor education is doing to our communities.

To gather the will of the people, we used an age-old American method: the referendum. In the sweeping, comprehensive National Referendum on Education, we collected Americans' best advice for how to fix the schools.

They told us they're ready to battle the real problems. They told us they're willing to sacrifice. They told us what to do. And they told us it's time to act—now.

Because everything depends on education.

FACING REALITY

Before we tried to solve the problems, we had to face up to the reality of the crisis: America's educational system—once the envy of the world—has crumbled.

In the past, Americans thrived on the knowledge that education was the key to the future. That each generation's children would be better off than their parents—because of education.

No more.

Declining performance. Scholastic Aptitude Test scores reveal a steady decline. Between 1963 and 1991, the median SAT scores plunged.[3]

- *Verbal:* from 478 to 422
- *Math:* from 502 to 474

The disturbing downward spiral was perhaps best described by the report of the National Commission on Excellence in Education: "For the first time in the history of the country, the education skills of one generation will not surpass, will not equal, will not even approach those of their parents."[4]

DON'T KNOW MUCH ABOUT HISTORY. . .

You don't have to search hard for evidence how severe the crisis is:

TEENS CAN'T READ

Nearly one in six seventeen-year-olds is functionally illiterate.[5] And one in ten Americans can't even read a McDonald's menu.[6]

ADULTS LACK BASIC SKILLS

The crisis isn't just a matter of performance in the classroom. A shocking proportion of young Americans—ages twenty-one to twenty-five—can't cope with the sort of everyday matters we've taken for granted:[7]

- How many can't read a bus schedule?
  - 97 percent of African-Americans
  - 93 percent of Hispanics
  - 75 percent of whites
- How many can't determine their change from a restaurant tab?
  - 92 percent of African-Americans
  - 80 percent of Hispanics
  - 56 percent of whites

A 1993 federal study showed that half of the nation's adults aren't proficient enough in English to write a letter about a billing error or calculate the length of a bus trip from a published schedule.[8]

WE'RE NOT PREPARING FOR THE TWENTY-FIRST CENTURY _____

In the new world economy, success is based on mastery of technology. That depends on a populace well versed in the basics of science and mathematics. But we're simply not doing the job.

- *Failing at math.* Less than half of America's high school seniors have a firm grasp of decimals, percents, fractions, and simple algebra.[9]
- *Shunning the sciences.* Only one in six high school students studies science beyond the tenth grade.[10]

BY ANY MEASURE, WE'RE FALLING BEHIND THE WORLD _____

The failures of the American educational system aren't just internal problems. They're at the root of our fading status in the world community. We simply can't measure up to our international competitors, because our population doesn't have the basic abilities.

Reading. Startling numbers of Americans pass through the schools without picking up the most important skill—the ability to read. How many finish school without reading skills?[11]

- Japan: 1 percent
- Germany: 4 percent
- United States: 13 percent

Geography. Our students are literally lost. They're less familiar with the world map than students in any other developed nation. For example: How many of sixteen major points can the average eighteen-year-old identify on a world map?[12]

- Germany: 11.2
- Japan: 9.5
- United States: 6.9

Science. Americans shy away from technical fields. Our high school students are among the least likely in the world to study advanced subjects like physics, advanced chemistry, and advanced biology.[13]

Math. Even our best students pale next to their foreign counterparts. In a mathematics test comparing the top 5 percent of American high school students to their counterparts in seven other countries, the United States ranked dead last.[14]

American students just don't stack up. In mathematics, the top *1 percent* of American high school seniors would place in the *fiftieth percentile* among Japanese students.[15]

It's no wonder that our college students aren't focusing on scientific fields: they simply lack the skills. What percentage of college graduates are scientists or engineers?

- Germany: 40 percent
- Japan: 40 percent
- United States: 15 percent[16]

A BAD REPORT CARD

Americans aren't naive. They know their education system is in a state of disaster. In assessing the situation, more than half of Americans give their public schools a grade of "C" or lower.[17] And the people who come in contact with students emerging from our schools have expressed growing alarm.

Frustrated bosses. More than three-quarters of employers say high school graduates don't have a good mastery of math, and only one in eight thinks they write well.[18]

Discouraged instructors. Three-quarters of college professors say undergraduates are seriously underprepared in basic skills.[19]

BEFORE SUCCESS: SURVIVAL

In the litany of problems plaguing the educational system, we haven't even mentioned the most pressing crisis in the nation's classrooms. Americans' top priority in straightening out their schools isn't improving math instruction or tackling literacy—it's ensuring the physical safety of our kids.

Cleaning up the schools. For all the lofty challenges facing educators, the first order of business is to make classrooms havens from the crime ravaging our cities.

- How many Americans say ridding the schools of drugs and violence is the top educational objective to achieve by the year 2000?
  - 63 percent[20]
- And how many say it's "very likely" we'll meet this goal?
  - 4 percent[21]

It's overwhelming: our public schools—and the teachers who work there—have taken on a survival mentality. The schools are so ravaged by crime that education is almost a secondary concern.

WHERE DID THE PROBLEMS COME FROM?

Despite the shocking litany of troubles that afflict our schools, we were determined to come up with a solution. And, as you'll see, the people came to the rescue of the education system with inspiration and conviction. But before we could even consider solutions, we had to further define the problem by examining a central question:

How did the situation get so dire? Where did we go wrong?

DO WE NEED TO SPEND MORE MONEY?

America's first approach to a problem is usually to spend money. But we found that the United States already doles out as much for education as the top spenders around the world.

- We allot a bigger chunk of our public money for education than Canada, the United Kingdom, or Germany.[22]
- We spend more of our gross domestic product on education than Japan or Germany.[23]
- We spend one-third more per pupil than Germany or Japan.[24]

In fact, education absorbs more of our nonfederal public money than anything else—one-third of all state and local tax money.

Quality keeps going down. But spending keeps going up.
How much did educational spending increase per capita?

- In the sixties: 57.7 percent
- In the seventies: 26.8 percent
- In the eighties: 28.7 percent[25]

In all, America's public school spending has nearly doubled since 1970.[26]

WHAT'S ALL THAT MONEY BUYING?

Those growing bills have paid for quantity, but not quality.

ENOUGH TEACHERS

Because we allot so much money to education, America has an ample supply of teachers working with our children. We have one teacher for every 17.3 students—a better rate than in Germany or the United Kingdom, and slightly lower than Japan's.[27]

ENOUGH BOOKS

American schoolchildren don't lack for reading material. In fact, they have access to the best-stocked school libraries in the world.[28]

ENOUGH HIGH-TECH EQUIPMENT

Our schools are well stocked with computers. In fact, a U.S. elementary school is three-and-a-half times more likely to have two or more computers for student use than a Japanese school.[29]

WHAT'S MISSING: MONEY CAN'T BUY ME EDUCATION

Obviously, if we're pouring as much material wealth—or more—into education as other countries, and we're not getting the same results, the problem must not be financial. So what is it? We found two basic problems at the core of our educational ills:

- Parents aren't involved in their children's education.
- Students don't work hard enough.

PARENTS DON'T CARE ENOUGH

Americans themselves realize the damage wrought by parents who aren't active parts of their children's learning. When Americans are asked to list the most serious problems with the public schools, the top answer—by far—is "lack of parental involvement."[30]

"You cannot talk about achieving 90-percent graduation rates without talking about parents who check on homework and turn off the television and know where their kids are," former education secretary Lamar Alexander has said.[31]

Who are the best teachers? The best role models? The best source of value? Mothers and fathers. Yet the nation's parents haven't taken that to heart.

Do parents participate in activities at their children's schools? How many parents have . . .

- . . . met with teachers or administrators about their own child?
  - 27 percent
- . . . attended a PTA meeting?
  - 14 percent
- . . . attended a school-board meeting?
  - 7 percent
- . . . had no involvement at all?
  - 49 percent[32]

STUDENTS DON'T WORK HARD ENOUGH

American students spend less time in the classroom than their counterparts around the globe.

Fewer school days. American students, with their long summer vacation and five-day school week, suffer from insufficient time in school.

How many days per year are students in school?[33]

- Japan: 243
- Germany: 240
- United Kingdom: 192
- United States: 180

Less homework. What's even more revealing than the length of the school year is the amount of work kids put into their learning. Study after study shows that American students simply don't put in the sort of effort that has become routine elsewhere.

What percentage of thirteen-year-olds spend at least two hours a day on homework?[34]

- Japan: 62 percent
- United Kingdom: 35 percent
- United States: 27 percent

In fact, the statistics are even more extreme: Japanese students spend as much as five times more hours on homework as Americans.[35]

More TV. American schoolchildren spend more than three times as many hours watching TV as studying.

What percentage of American eighth graders spend . . .

- . . . less than an hour a day on homework?
  - 73 percent
- . . . more than three hours a day watching TV?
  - 81 percent

WHAT ARE THE KEYS TO REFORMING EDUCATION?

What's missing from the schools? Essentially, the nation's education system *isn't a system at all,* but a potpourri of school districts with no particular direction and no coordinated programs. For too long, school districts have let mediocrity and declining performance go unchecked.

America lacks a national vision for education.

It's time to stop the decline. It's time to remake our schools—to make them the best in the world. That will require an integrated, thoughtful approach—one that doesn't take anything for granted.

Once we identified the major, pervasive elements harming education, we moved on to discover specific ailments—the particular weaknesses and faults that require remedies. When we looked at efforts to reform education, and demands to upgrade the system, the problems fell into eight categories.

We pinpointed eight major challenges facing education. For each issue, we explored a solution, considering its benefits, its drawbacks, and how the American people might respond to the proposed reforms.

THE EDUCATION EIGHT: WHAT NEEDS FIXING IN AMERICA'S SCHOOLS

1. *Parental apathy:* Parents aren't involved in their kids' education.
2. *Student performance:* Students pass through school without learning enough.
3. *Curriculum:* The quality and breadth of American education is inconsistent.
4. *National control:* There's no national control over the schools.
5. *School hours:* Students don't spend enough time learning.
6. *Teaching:* The quality of teachers is declining.
7. *Red tape:* The cost and effort of administration is stifling the schools.
8. *Vocational training:* There's no track for the 75 percent of students who aren't bound for college degrees.

MEETING THE CHALLENGES

CHALLENGE NO. 1: PARENTS AREN'T INVOLVED IN THEIR CHILDREN'S EDUCATION _____

Most children today live in families where one or both parents work full-time—or with only one parent. With the stresses and time demands of working lives, parents don't have the hours or the energy to take active roles in their children's educational lives. Yet without parental activism, no innovations in education can work.

The solution: Give parents a choice of where to send their children to school.

A voucher system would allow parents to send their children to any public, private, or parochial school. This would empower parents and place more responsibility on them for the quality of their children's education.

What the people say: How many Americans supported a voucher system to provide school choice?[36]

- In 1970: 43 percent
- In 1991: 50 percent

THE PROS

Better consumers. Choice would create a free market for education: If parents had to choose their children's schools, they would become more informed consumers, immediately becoming more active and involved in the educational process. They would be forced to decide what they want their children to learn, to find the schools that are most suitable, and then to monitor the development of both child and school.

More responsible schools. The concept also would make schools more accountable. With a more open approach, the best schools would attract more students, the less attractive ones fewer.

THE CONS

An uninformed public. In reality, most parents don't know enough about educational options to make informed decisions for their children. What do parents say they know about schools in their communities?[37]

- Enough to make the best choice for a child: 51 percent
- Very little or nothing at all: 33 percent

Inaction. Even with the option to choose, most parents say they would opt to keep their children in their present schools. In fact, Minnesota has allowed students to choose any public school since 1988—but only 1 percent have switched.[38]

Weaker public schools. Opponents of the voucher system maintain that providing government incentives for students to attend private schools would undermine the very integrity of the public school system, which has historically been one of the nation's great strengths.

CHALLENGE NO. 2: STUDENTS PASS THROUGH SCHOOL WITHOUT LEARNING ENOUGH

Our educational system has come to accept mediocrity and failure as integral parts of the process. Too many students move through our schools from one level to the next without anything to show for their experience. In essence, there is no quality control—nothing to make sure students actually accomplish anything in the classroom.

The solution: Require students to pass minimum competency examinations at all levels of education.

These tests would assess students at the primary, secondary, college entry, and college levels to ensure that students have acquired the skills and knowledge to succeed at the next level.

THE PROS
These tests would empower students and add integrity to the educational system by making sure that any student at a given grade level belongs at that level. Currently, grade levels have little practical meaning, and students know they can slip through without effort.

THE CONS
Teachers and principals would lose autonomy in making decisions about students' grade levels. Further, this solution might penalize students for the failures of their teachers.

CHALLENGE NO. 3: THE QUALITY AND BREADTH OF AMERICAN EDUCATION IS INCONSISTENT _____

Education varies so much from state to state and from district to district that there's no consistent body of knowledge to teach American school-children. The educational system lacks coordinated national objectives.

The solution: Create a standardized, national core curriculum.

A coordinated, comprehensive national classroom agenda would designate specific, substantive areas of study and require that all schools teach them and bring their students to certain levels of performance in those areas. The plan would provide for national standards in basic areas like math, science, English, and the social sciences.

What the people say: More than two-thirds of Americans favor creating a standardized, national curriculum for the public schools.[39]

What percentage of Americans said we should require all schools to meet national achievement standards?[40]

- In 1989: 70 percent
- In 1991: 81 percent

THE PROS
A uniform curriculum would bring order and national objectives to the hodgepodge of programs that now exist in our schools. The result would be a population with shared knowledge and comparable skills.

THE CONS
Introducing national standards usurps power from local school districts, and adds constraints to school boards, administrators, and teachers, who are already working to live up to state and locally imposed standards. Advocates of local control say teachers and administrators are best equipped to decide what their students ought to be learning—not the federal government.

CHALLENGE NO. 4: THERE'S NO NATIONAL CONTROL OVER SCHOOLS

Our educational system doesn't measure results. It's impossible for parents to gauge how well their children and schools stack up within the district, the state, or the country.

Solution: Require standardized tests to assess all students' performance.

Testing is the best way to determine whether our schools are effective. With exams, parents, educators, and policy makers could check the results of their efforts. With a national core curriculum in place, the tests could measure not "aptitude"—which current tests gauge—but actual learning. Japan, Germany, and other nations have successfully used such tests in their education systems.

What the people say: Americans show overwhelming support for the idea of testing students. They think tests tell the full story.

What percentage support testing in . . .[41]

- . . . core subjects? 88 percent
- . . . problem-solving skills? 84 percent
- . . . writing skills? 85 percent

THE PROS

Academic achievement tests would bring improvement rapidly. Schools need a quality-control system to create a reference point, demonstrating where schools need to improve. It would make educators accountable for their performance. Rewards would go to successful districts and states, and those with poor test results could refocus their efforts to improve their programs.

THE CONS

America has a strong tradition of local control of education. The nation's fifty thousand school boards are wary of national mandates, and many local educators resist reforms that come from the outside. National standards would raise the threshold too high for some districts, and would prove too mediocre for others.

CHALLENGE NO. 5: STUDENTS DON'T SPEND ENOUGH TIME LEARNING _____

The average American student spends 810 hours per year in active learning—that is, in class, or doing homework. And the average Japanese student? More than 1,940 hours.[42] Americans' short school days and long summer vacations mean that, in very simple terms, U.S. students have less chance to learn than their counterparts in other countries.

Solution: Lengthen the school year and the school day.

Extending the school day would ensure that students would spend more of their time in a supervised, active learning environment.

The American school year is among the shortest in the developed world (sixty-three days shorter than Japan's). Adding several weeks of learning would bring the United States into conformity with the rest of the world.

What the people say: There is growing support for adding time to the school year and day.

How many Americans support extending the school year?[43]

- In 1982: 37 percent
- In 1991: 51 percent

How many Americans support extending the school day?[44]

- In 1982: 37 percent
- In 1991: 46 percent

THE PROS

Simply put, with more time to learn, students would learn more. And longer days would ensure that children (especially with parents working outside the home) are spending their hours in a learning environment, rather than on the streets.

THE CONS

Adding learning hours and days would add costs to an already overburdened system. It would require that school facilities be kept open for more days in the year, as well as more hours each day.

CHALLENGE NO. 6: THE QUALITY OF TEACHERS IS DECLINING_____

In recent decades, teaching has lost its attraction as a profession. It was once one of the only professions that welcomed highly educated women. But as more and more professional arenas have opened up to women, fewer and fewer of the brightest, most promising young people have chosen to become teachers. Other realms offer better pay and benefits and more respect. As a result, the quality of teachers has plunged.

A case in point: more than half of America's high school principals say their math teachers aren't qualified to teach mathematics in their schools.[45]

Solutions:

- *Improve teacher training and recruitment*
- *Require competency exams for teachers*
- *Pay teachers more*

Training and recruitment. Schools would open alternative paths to the profession—besides the traditional teaching schools. This would encourage individuals with experience in business, technology, and other fields—not just education—to enter the classroom. In addition, teacher-training programs would raise their entrance and graduation requirements to improve the quality of people entering the field.

Competency exams. More and more states are requiring teachers to pass competency exams before being certified. Ten states required the exams in 1980, but the number was up to forty-four by the end of the decade.[46]

Better pay. Money talks: good salaries will attract good teachers and bring prestige and status to the profession. American teachers are paid far worse than their colleagues in other developed nations.

How much is the average teacher paid?[47]

- In Switzerland: $53,900
- In Japan: $44,200
- In Germany: $34,000
- In the United States: $26,000

What the people say: Americans express fairly strong support for raising pay to attract better teachers.

How many say . . .[48]

- ... teachers should be paid more?
    - 54 percent
- ... effective teachers should receive extra pay?
    - 69 percent

THE PROS

For too long, schools have relied on sheer goodwill to motivate teachers to work in the schools. In order to teach, people have had to sacrifice more lucrative and prestigious careers. Increasing pay—and adding other incentives to the recruitment process—would bring a free-market approach to attracting better-quality applicants to teaching positions.

THE CONS

Teachers' unions and other groups have consistently opposed competency tests because they emphasize random areas of knowledge and don't take into consideration the value of classroom experience for effective teaching. States that impose the tests have had difficulty with long-term professionals, who resent the implication that they may not be competent.

And increasing teacher pay across the board may create an extreme financial burden on school districts and state governments. The high cost of a higher pay scale would require new approaches to financing public education.

CHALLENGE NO. 7: THE COST AND EFFORT OF ADMINISTRATION IS STIFLING THE SCHOOLS _____

Our education system spends too much on bureaucracy and not enough on educating people. Educational bureaucracies have become bloated.

The solution: Cut the bureaucracy and empower the schools.

More tax dollars would go to the classroom, and fewer would go to national and local education bureaucracies. More money—and more power—would go to principals and teachers, the people who have the most direct impact on learning.

Many of the "brass tack" reforms education experts call for—such as school-based management—give more power to educational professionals, taking it away from administrators.

What the people say: Americans show support for keeping control of schools at home. Seventy-six percent of Americans say principals and teachers should have more say about running schools than district administrators or school boards.[49] And 72 percent say local school authorities should have more say in how federal school dollars are spent.[50]

PROS

The approach encourages local creativity, which may lead to the best quality. Studies show that the best schools are good for idiosyncratic reasons. Quality has more to do with teamwork, a sense of mission, and a strong principal than with standards imposed from outside. In fact, the best learning environments are often innately defiant of bureaucratic efforts to control them.

CONS

Giving too much control to schools and local districts can be damaging; it may allow some schools to flourish, while elsewhere, students become the victims of poor management and poor quality of teaching. The idea may benefit the few (in areas with strong parental involvement and exceptional principals), but detract from the many (those in less well-equipped schools who then lack the benefit of a strong district or state administration).

CHALLENGE NO. 8: THERE'S NO TRACK FOR THE 75 PERCENT OF STUDENTS WHO DON'T PLAN TO GRADUATE FROM COLLEGE

Only about one in four Americans receives a college degree. Yet the nation has failed to direct its attention toward the other three-quarters of the population. We have no coordinated, national system for training people for nonprofessional jobs.

The solution: a national system of worker training.

Many developed countries benefit from strong worker-training programs that result from partnerships between business and government. In Germany, for example, students who don't plan to attend college—

about 70 percent of all students—enter school-industry apprenticeship programs at age fifteen or sixteen. After three years, after passing competence exams, they become "journeymen" with known skill levels. (Thirty percent of Germany's educational spending goes to the apprenticeship programs.)

EDUCATION BY THE PEOPLE, FOR THE PEOPLE: THE FIRST NATIONAL REFERENDUM ON EDUCATION

How should we fix education? Once we had assessed the problems and looked at the reforms being discussed by so-called education experts, it was time to move on to the real experts.

We went to the people.

We knew that Americans had a strong resolve about how to mend the ailing education system. And we made it our job to tap into that resolve, and discover what the people already knew.

How much are citizens willing to sacrifice? How radically should the nation reform its system? How much federal control and coordination is needed? What is in the best interest of our children?

To answer those questions and delineate a national agenda, we asked a variety of Americans to "vote" on a comprehensive group of reforms that have been put forth to address the issues in education. We knew the answers wouldn't be random responses to polls on various issues, but a comprehensive, national approach to educating our children.

THE QUESTIONS

I. National Competency Standards for Students
    Institute and enforce nationwide competency requirements for students at all levels of education. Require students to meet standards before progressing to subsequent academic levels or receiving diplomas.

Favor [ ]   Oppose [ ]

II. National Core Curriculum
Establish a common national core curriculum in English, math, science, history, and other basic areas. Develop national standardized tests to measure students' progress in each core subject.

Favor [ ]   Oppose [ ]

III. Longer School Day
Extend the school day to seven hours, bringing the length of the American school day into conformity with the longer days preferred by other countries.

Favor [ ]   Oppose [ ]

IV. Longer School Year
Add days to the school year and shorten the summer break, to bring the American school year into conformity with the longer years preferred by other countries.

Favor [ ]   Oppose [ ]

V. Mandatory Parental Participation
Mandate the active participation of parents in the education of their children. Require parents to visit their children's schools, to monitor closely their children's progress, and to participate in schoolwork with their children.

Favor [ ]   Oppose [ ]

VI. Universal School Choice
Devise a "voucher" system to allow parents to choose any school for their children—public, private, or parochial. Allow parents to take their children out of bad schools and enroll them in good schools regardless of area or income.

Favor [ ]   Oppose [ ]

VII.   Choice—Only Within Public Schools
Allow parents to send their children to any public school—
but don't extend it to private schools.

Favor [   ]   Oppose [   ]

VIII.   Raise Teachers' Pay
Raise teachers' salaries—even if it requires higher taxes—to
help attract more qualified individuals to the profession and
to help retain good teachers.

Favor [   ]   Oppose [   ]

IX.   Competency Examinations for Teachers
Require teachers to pass stringent competency tests. Base
tenure and promotions on a balanced combination of se-
niority, classroom performance, and participation in contin-
ual training.

Favor [   ]   Oppose [   ]

X.   Limits on Bureaucracy
Mandate that school districts limit the size and scope of their
nonteaching bureaucratic staffs. Require them to allot a specific minimum percentage of all education money to actual
classroom costs.

Favor [   ]   Oppose [   ]

XI.   Increased Authority for Teachers and Principals
Give teachers and principals more authority in making educational choices for their schools. Control and reduce the
power of school superintendents, school boards, and other
bodies.

Favor [   ]   Oppose [   ]

XII.   National Vocational Training Program
Launch a comprehensive, national vocational training program for those not planning to attend college—perhaps as a
partnership between government and business.

Favor [   ]   Oppose [   ]

THE PEOPLE SPEAK... ☆
ON EDUCATION

☆

1. PARENTAL INVOLVEMENT: YES _____

Most Americans realize that education starts at home. Children read clearly the messages they get from their parents. Without the support and involvement of mothers and fathers, education has little chance for success.

- *79 percent* of Americans say parents should be required to participate in their children's education.

CHOICE: YES
Even without requiring parental involvement, it's possible to encourage parents to take an active interest in their children's education. How? By giving parents a choice of where to send their children to school. The idea: When parents are forced to make basic educational decisions, they'll pay closer attention to how the schools are performing. And if schools aren't doing well, they won't get the support of parents.

- *98 percent* of Americans support some kind of school choice.

THE BREAKDOWN
- How many support universal choice (vouchers to apply to parochial or public schools)?
  - 56 percent
- How many opt for giving students a choice among public schools?
  - 42 percent

2. STUDENT ACCOUNTABILITY: YES _____

Are students merely the victims of a poor educational system? Or do they have some responsibility for their own progress?

114

Most Americans want to hold students accountable for what they learn in school. For all the effort and money we put into education, we want to make sure that students are getting something out of it.

- *88 percent* of Americans favor national student competency standards.

3. A NATIONAL CURRICULUM: YES

Should what you learn in school depend on where you go to school? Americans say: No.

- *88 percent* of Americans support the establishment of a national core curriculum.

What would we gain from such a program? A coordinated, comprehensive, national classroom agenda—in math, science, English, history, and social studies—would ensure that students would receive comprehensive and useful educations, no matter where they live. It would allow for flexibility and creativity beyond the minimum, but it would address the growing issues of ignorance and illiteracy that are plaguing our country.

4. MANDATORY STANDARDIZED TESTING: YES

How do we know whether our schools are doing their jobs?

- *88 percent* of Americans support requiring standardized tests.

With a national curriculum in place, standardized tests could measure not just "aptitude" but learning. Such a tool would enable educators to evaluate teachers, schools, districts, and states. Standardized tests—if they're meaningful and well developed—are the best way to bring quality control to the educational system at every level.

5. MORE TIME IN SCHOOL: YES

The formula couldn't be simpler: The more time you spend in school—in hours, in days, in months—the more you learn.

- *62 percent* of Americans support extending the school day. And *60 percent* favor adding days to the school year.

Americans are well aware that their children are falling behind the rest of the world in education. The conclusion: Increasing the quantity will lead to better quality.

6. GREATER INCENTIVES AND HIGHER STANDARDS FOR TEACHERS: YES _____

Anyone who's ever been to school knows that the better the teaching, the better the learning.

What's the best way to increase the quality of the teachers in American schools? We approached the problem from two angles—standards and incentives—finding ways to attract the best people, and then making sure they perform well.

Americans are more enthusiastic about competency tests than about paying teachers more—perhaps because higher pay would mean higher taxes.

- *94 percent* support stringent competency tests for teachers.
- *56 percent* support raising pay for teachers.

7. CUT THE BUREAUCRACY AND EMPOWER THE SCHOOLS: YES _____

As much as Americans support education, they loathe bureaucracy. They state in clear terms that resources ought to go to teaching students, not administering the schools, not keeping bureaucracy going. Just teaching.

- *98 percent* of Americans support requiring districts to limit the size and power of nonteaching staffs and to focus at least a minimum amount on classroom costs.
- *74 percent* support increasing the authority of teachers and principals over school boards and other educational boards.

8. CREATE A NATIONAL VOCATIONAL TRACK: YES ___

Three in four students never graduate from college, yet we're virtually alone in the world in our dearth of programs to give these people occupational skills. Americans say enough is enough. It's time to get moving on this vital issue.

- *89 percent* of Americans support a comprehensive, national vocational-training program for students who don't plan to graduate from college.

A RESOLVE TO ACT

More than on virtually any other issue, we found a resolve among the American people that it's time to act—time to do *something* about education. The nearly unanimous support for virtually every variety of reform indicates a phenomenal sense of the importance of education. Americans respond that it is so vital that it underlies every other issue we discuss in this book. It's time to take action.

HEALTH CARE

MYTH: America is the healthiest nation on earth.

FACT: We're not even in the top fifteen.

As we head toward the twenty-first century, the United States is a nation in failing health. The conventional wisdom says Americans take better care of themselves and have access to better medical care than people anywhere else.

It's simply not true.

With all its effort on the issue—Hillary Clinton's five-hundred-member task force, a special presidential address, and an unprecedented push in Congress—the White House hasn't come close to solving the problem. Even the most ardent supporters of President Clinton's plan admit that it can't do everything to bring adequate health care to every American.

All the hoopla has served only to accentuate the crisis.

By objective standards, our health is flagging. In the two most crucial indicators of public health—life expectancy and infant mortality—the United States is steadily falling behind.

- *Shorter lives.* In longevity, the United States ranks sixteenth, behind countries like Cyprus, Greece, and Hong Kong.
- *Infant death.* America ranks twenty-fifth in the world in infant mortality, behind the likes of Singapore, Ireland, and Spain.

Millions of Americans can't afford to go to the doctor. While the nation's top hospitals and research centers lunge forward with cutting-edge treatments and high-tech breakthroughs, millions of citizens are left out in the cold.

- *Left out.* About 37 million Americans—15 percent of the population—have no medical insurance.
- *Vulnerable.* Another 60 million don't have health insurance to protect them in case of serious illness.[1]

118

America is the ONLY developed country besides South Africa without a universal health-care plan covering every citizen.

That leaves millions of Americans—both poor and middle class—with no way to pay their medical bills. And it has a wider impact, dictating our actions at every turn: millions are afraid to leave their jobs, for fear of losing medical coverage; older Americans live in fear of unpredictable medical expenses that could leave them penniless; businesses are financially stifled by the growing cost of insuring their employees.

How should we pay to take care of ourselves? For decades, Americans have accepted a costly bureaucratic hodgepodge as a necessity of life.

But no more.

Ninety percent of Americans think the nation's health-care programs need overhauling. And two in five say the system should be completely rebuilt.[2]

But how to do that?

DON'T WE HAVE THE WORLD'S BEST MEDICINE?

If you're rich, America is the best place in the world to get sick.

This is the home of the artificial heart and of TPA, the miracle heart-attack remedy. American doctors have even come up with a cure for baldness. The nation's hospitals and research centers undisputedly lead the world in medical research, technology, and treatments.

The United States has more highly trained, specialized surgeons than anywhere in the world. The nation's 2,107 cardiovascular surgeons—more than in the rest of the world combined—do more than 350,000 bypass operations a year.

The nation so overflows with specialists that world-class medicine is available no matter where you live. Kansas City, Missouri—a city of 1.6 million—has fourteen hospitals that perform heart surgery. Toronto, with more than twice the population, has five.

Even the most advanced procedures are commonplace here. More than two thousand people receive heart transplants each year—compared to Japan's *zero*. Over 150 American hospitals perform organ transplants, compared to 11 in Canada and in Japan, *zero*.

And America remains a world leader in creating and selling medical products. In 1990, the United States exported more than $11 billion in medical equipment and drugs—up from $4 billion in 1983.[3]

U.S. hospitals are outfitted with the best equipment available. American hospitals have more than two thousand MRIs (magnetic resonance imagers), which take crisp, clear pictures of the brain. (Price tag: $2 million.) Canada has fifteen.

Finally, U.S. hospitals have room for sick people. While hospitals all over the world are overcrowded, admitting only the sickest patients, America has more hospital beds per person than any other nation—and 35 percent of them are vacant.

WITH ALL THOSE RESOURCES, WHY AREN'T WE HEALTHIER?

If every American could afford to visit any doctor—to check into any hospital, to seek the best prenatal care and the top geriatric care—we'd be a well-cared-for, physically fit nation. The great problem of American health care isn't technology or research. It's access.

Too many of us simply can't pay for care.

Some 37 million Americans—15 percent of the population—have no medical insurance. Another 60 million lack enough insurance to cover a serious illness. And in any two-year period, 30 million more go without coverage for long stretches of time.[4]

Each year, 15 million people are turned away by doctors and hospitals because they can't afford to pay.[5]

The group most lacking in coverage is the one that's the most vulnerable: children.

One in three uninsured Americans is a child. A quarter of America's young lack health insurance coverage.

The implications of those facts are shocking for a modern world power: nearly a third of preschoolers—three-quarters in some cities—haven't received routine childhood vaccinations.[6]

The uninsured aren't on the fringes of society; they're in our midst.

Two-thirds of uninsured Americans have jobs. And 70 percent of those lacking medical insurance are above the poverty line.[7]

AREN'T WE PUTTING ENOUGH MONEY INTO HEALTH CARE?

The troubling picture of American health care—with its built-in injustices and its failure to protect millions upon millions of citizens—hasn't come about for a lack of spending.

The United States puts more money into health care than any other nation on earth. We spend 40 percent more on medical care than Canada; 90 percent more than Germany; and twice as much as Japan.[8] Each year, America spends $2,354 per capita for health care; Great Britain spends $836.[9]

The United States spent a shocking $738 billion on health care in 1991—about *12 percent of the gross domestic product,* up from less than 5 percent in the early 1960s. We spend twice for medical care what we do for defense—and 50 percent more than for education.

Health-care costs are skyrocketing—jumping by 20 percent a year.[10] The health-care bill will rise to 17 percent of the gross national product by the year 2000. (Health care alone will exceed the combined costs of national defense, education, and recreation.) By 2030, medical costs could eat up 26 percent of the GNP each year.[11]

Medical bills are rising at twice the annual inflation rate.[12] And soaring medical bills mean Americans have less money to pay their other expenses. Take-home pay hasn't really risen since the early 1970s, largely because of the soaring medical-insurance bills and the growing share of taxes needed for government health programs.

WHY DOES HEALTH CARE COST SO MUCH?

In the process of looking after our health, the United States wastes about $200 billion a year.[13] For six primary reasons, our health-care costs have spiraled out of control:

1. *Administrative waste.* Too much money is spent on bureaucracy instead of caring for people. The United States spends twenty-three cents out of every health-care dollar on administrative costs.

America's 1,500 insurance companies use a jumble of claim forms to pay 6,000 hospitals and 600,000 physicians. The result: $75 billion annually in bureaucratic paperwork waste.[14]

In fact, the number of health-care administrators is rising three times faster than the number of doctors.

2. *Lack of restraint on physicians.* In the 1970s and '80s, few restraints limited doctors' practices and prices. American physicians were trained to use the latest and costliest equipment, drugs, and procedures, and they earned more than their colleagues anywhere else in the world.[15] (Today, the average American physician makes $150,000 per year.) *Doctors' annual income is rising 50 percent faster than the national average.*

3. *Too many hospital beds.* The American hospital occupancy rate is 65 percent, compared to 87 percent in Germany and 81 percent in Canada.

4. *"Defensive medicine."* As malpractice suits have become commonplace, physicians have paid as much attention to avoiding lawsuits as to healing patients. Three out of four doctors order more tests than are medically needed, because they're wary of malpractice charges.[16] *These "defensive" practices add as much as $50 billion annually to the cost of health care.*[17]

5. *High-tech obsession.* American doctors have made high-tech medicine—rather than preventive care—their focal point.

6. *Unnecessary treatment.* The system gives American doctors financial incentives to do as many procedures as possible. *In fact, one-third of the medical procedures performed in the United States may not be medically required.*

Moreover, millions of Americans carry unlimited insurance, and those patients are more likely to opt for elective surgery.

HOW DO WE PAY THE MEDICAL BILLS?

American consumers say they have more trouble paying for health care than for any other expense item.[18]

More and more, individual Americans are facing the burden of paying their own medical bills. Nearly two-thirds of those with employer health plans say they pay a bigger chunk of their medical bills now than two years ago.[19]

Eighty-eight percent of Americans footed some part of their own health-care bill—out-of-pocket—in 1991; 39 percent paid more than $1,000.[20]

With money tight all around, how can we afford to cover ever-growing medical bills? More than half of consumers are forced to take money from savings to pay doctors' bills.[21] One in six must get a loan or go into debt.[22]

Sometimes, there's simply no money to pay. *Four in ten Americans skip seeing doctors for medical problems because it costs too much.*[23]

In fact, worries about medical costs have become so pervasive that they control our lives. Thirty percent of Americans say they have held on to jobs they wanted to quit—or had someone in their household do so—because they didn't want to lose health coverage.[24]

HOW DID IT GET THIS WAY?

The United States doesn't have a health-care *system.*

Rather, we have a chaotic health-care marketplace—a patchwork of government and private sources crudely stitched together to attempt to cover the diverse medical needs of the nation. Four times in this century, reformers have come close to enacting a national health-care plan.

Without success.

What has evolved instead is an awkward meeting of capitalism and socialism: private insurance and government assistance.

PRIVATE INSURANCE

In 1940, fewer than one in ten U.S. citizens had health insurance.

By 1980, more than 82 percent of Americans were covered—mostly by private health-care plans provided by employers.

The federal government encouraged people to buy health insurance by making employer medical plans tax-free. In fact, the incentives were so appealing that many workers ended up with an excess of insurance.[25]

The upside: For several decades, private insurance appealed to both companies and workers. For employers, health plans promoted company loyalty; for workers, employer plans saved them money—in premiums and tax dollars—over personal plans.

The downside: What was once a benevolent fringe benefit has spiraled out of control to become a crippling expense, siphoning billions from the nation's economy:

- In 1989, American companies spent $173 billion on health-care coverage for their employees—a sum equal to their total net profits.[26]
- Businesses' share of health-care costs has risen from *17 percent* in 1965 to more than *30 percent* today.
- The cost of insurance and medical bills per employee soared from $1,700 in 1985 to $3,200 in 1990 (and may exceed $15,000 per employee by 2000).[27]

Who pays? The worker. Many employers have shifted the burden of health-care costs to workers, raising their premiums and the portion of costs that come out of employees' pockets.

One in five companies that offered health insurance for workers in 1980 has dropped health insurance programs altogether.[28]

MEDICARE AND MEDICAID

In 1965, Congress approved two new programs designed to increase Americans' ability to afford adequate health care:

- *Disabled and elderly.* Medicare, financed by the federal government, provides a minimum level of health insurance for the disabled and those over sixty-five.
- *Poor.* Medicaid uses state and federal dollars, disbursed by the states, to offer coverage to the destitute.

Under each system, hospitals and doctors bill the government for care. Medicare patients pay a small portion of their bills, and Medicaid patients pay nothing.

As costs for the programs exploded, Medicare shifted in 1983 to a new reimbursement system, known as "prospective payment," to reduce hospital costs. Under that plan, the government listed hundreds of diagnoses and treatments and specified the amount Medicare would pay for each.

The upside: Under the plans, medical care is available to millions of poor and elderly Americans who previously went without.

The downside:

- Millions don't fall within the programs' categories, and can't afford private insurance. They are left without coverage. (Medicaid covers just 40 percent of those in poverty.)
- The bureaucratic paperwork of Medicare and Medicaid is overwhelming. It costs hospitals $75 million annually to photocopy medical records to be sent to Medicare officials.[29]
- Many hospitals have reacted to Medicare's "prospective payment" system by jacking up prices for services that don't fall within the government's guidelines.

PRESSURES OF THE NINETIES

To make matters worse, three new factors make the health-care crisis even more pressing.

The uninsured underclass. The needs of millions in poverty have severe effects on health care. Each year, 375,000 drug-exposed babies are born, often requiring $200,000 or more to keep each child alive.

The AIDS epidemic. Young adults—historically among the healthiest Americans—are now running up astronomical health-care bills as a result of acquired immune deficiency syndrome. The United States currently spends about $7 billion annually to care for the 175,000 people with AIDS. Experts estimate that over one million people now have the virus and will contract the disease.[30]

The graying of America. The aged have the greatest health-care needs, and their growing numbers are stretching health-care programs to the breaking point. Medicare, the program aiding the elderly, is growing so fast it will outstrip the defense budget by 2005.

The number of adults aged seventy-five or over has increased from 5.6 million thirty years ago to 13.2 million today. By 2020, when the first baby boomers reach this frontier, 21 million Americans will be seventy-five or over.

WHAT WILL HAPPEN TO THE AVERAGE CONSUMER?

The medical crisis is felt in every American household. It's not merely a distant, theoretical issue bandied about by politicians; it's wreaking havoc on every home, where anxious consumers worry about taking care of themselves and their children.

Two out of five Americans say they don't have adequate medical coverage.[31] More than three-quarters say they're not adequately covered in case of a permanent, disabling illness or accident.[32]

With figures like those, it's understandable that Americans are more and more worried about their ability to get health care for themselves and their families:

- 71 percent worry they won't be able to afford adequate health care.[33]
- 59 percent fear they won't have enough money or insurance to pay for long-term care when they're elderly.[34]
- 48 percent worry that they won't be able to pay for their health-care costs *in the next year.*[35]

WILL AMERICANS WAIT FOR SOLUTIONS?

Those sorts of concerns have made the health-care issue—which has quietly simmered for decades beneath the surface—rise in the American consciousness.

Now, it's ready to explode.

Once a question touching only the poor and disenfranchised, the medical-care situation has grown into a pressing problem affecting nearly every American household.

- 91 percent of Americans believe there is a crisis in health care in America.
- 93 percent of consumers feel that health-care costs are higher than they should be.

- Only one in three Americans is satisfied with the health care provided by insurance companies—a sixteen-year low.[36]

Voters are taking those opinions to the polls. In 1991, Pennsylvania voters chose Harris Wofford for the U.S. Senate, based almost entirely on his support of health-care reform. And 91 percent of registered voters said that health-care policy would be important in determining their choice in the 1992 presidential race.[37]

A CLASS STRUGGLE?

A primary reason for the increased public concern about health care is that middle-class Americans—the vast majority of the population—feel more and more vulnerable. Many people who once assumed that the system protected them have begun to feel threatened, as private insurance companies refine their methods of avoiding those with the highest risks.

Increasingly, middle-class Americans feel that they're subject to the same health-care insecurities as the uninsured poor. This vulnerability has changed the political dimensions of the issue: Americans are far more concerned about stopping runaway costs than providing access to health care for their needier fellow citizens.

What's the biggest problem with health care? Forty-seven percent of Americans said cost; only 22 percent said lack of access.[38]

SOLUTIONS: WHAT CAN WE DO?

Americans view the breakdown of health care as a failure of the democratic system: Eight in ten Americans agree that health care is a basic right that the government should guarantee.[39]

The pressing question: *How?*

The beginning of the answer is: money. Taxpayers accept the idea that it will cost money to overhaul the health-care system. *Eighty percent of Americans say government spending on health care should increase.*[40]

Specifically, most Americans support a national health-care plan with coverage for every citizen—and they think higher taxes should support such a plan. *Seventy percent of U.S. citizens believe the government should provide health insurance to all Americans who can't afford it, even if this would require higher taxes.*[41]

Despite the demand for government programs, when it comes to their own tax bills, Americans seem less enthusiastic about pitching in. How much would taxpayers be willing to up their own share of annual taxes to provide care to the 37 million uninsured Americans?

Nearly one-third say: *Nothing.*

And another third say they wouldn't pay over fifty dollars more per year.[42]

WILL AMERICANS ACCEPT TRADE-OFFS?

We worry about getting coverage for everyone. But more than that, we worry about getting the best care in the world for ourselves when we're sick.

As much as we clamor for reform, we like some of what we have. The toughest hurdle for any proposed reform may be Americans' stubbornness about giving up the advantages they now have.

- 62 percent wouldn't give up costly treatments like organ transplants to lower costs.[43]
- 54 percent wouldn't give up choosing their own physician to lower medical costs.[44]
- 46 percent would not be willing to wait longer to see a doctor if it meant lowering medical costs.[45]

HEALTH CARE REFORM: HOW FAR SHOULD WE GO?

Socialized Medicine.

For decades, those two words have struck terror in the hearts of many Americans. They conjure up notions of a massive, inefficient muddle, implying that Americans have turned their backs on capitalist values to create a new, cumbersome bureaucracy.

Would that be the case? Every other developed nation—except for South Africa—adopted universal health-care plans long ago. Our health standards continue to slip, our medical spending to swell.

Yet we don't change.

UNIVERSAL CARE: WHAT'S THE APPEAL?

Why have we opted out of the mainstream? And why has the idea of universal care caught on nearly unanimously everywhere in the world?

Two trends stand out:

- *High cost.* The United States spends far more on health care than any other country—an expense that has not resulted in a healthier society.
- *Low care.* More citizens go without medical care—and more are dissatisfied with their care—in the United States than in countries with national health insurance.

The common concern is that universal care is a boondoggle, a costly bureaucracy that would cripple the nation. Yet the United States now spends more than 12 percent of its gross national product on health care—more than any country with universal care.

Universal plans save money by streamlining health care. They cut administrative costs; they let the state control health expenses; they do away with costly, unnecessary, or redundant treatments.

There's a trade-off. While countries with universal systems benefit from having access for all their citizens, they're less likely to be centers for advanced research: the system simply lacks the free-market incentives for research and development.

HOW DO THEY DO IT ELSEWHERE?

How have other countries tackled the problem? Looking abroad to the health-care experience of other nations may help Americans find solutions at home.

Canada. Canadian taxpayers pay 10 percent of their incomes toward the national health plan. Doctors and hospitals are private, but they negotiate fees and budgets with the provincial governments, which provide insurance for all their citizens. Patients choose their own doctors and hospitals, who charge the government on a set payment schedule.

A recent survey found that 56 percent of Canadians are satisfied, overall, with their health-care system, compared to just 10 percent of Americans.

Germany. Germans can go to the doctors and hospitals of their choice, and pay nothing but a small charge for drugs. What pays for their health care? A payroll tax on workers and their employers (like our Social Security tax). The taxes go into a thousand local "sickness funds"—similar to health maintenance organizations—which bargain with regional medical groups over services and fees.

Surveys show that Germans are much happier with their health-care system than are Canadians or Americans.[46]

Japan. Japan's health-care system is marked by its intensity of competition. Two-thirds of all Japanese health-care costs are paid for by employers; the government runs health insurance plans for small businesses and retirees. The money is pooled into sickness funds, like Germany's, which compete with hospitals and clinics.

The Japanese have the world's longest life expectancy and lowest infant-mortality rates—yet they spend less on health care than Americans, Germans, or Canadians.

WHAT ARE OUR OPTIONS?

While most Americans agree that our health-care system needs reform, a consensus has not arisen about what form the changes ought to take. The debate centers on two questions:

- *Piecemeal or wholesale?* Should we scrap the system and start over, or slightly alter the status quo?
- *Capitalist or socialist?* Should we change through a *free-market* approach—bringing more competition—or *social-welfare* principles, calling for more state intervention and control?

The four most-discussed alternatives for solving the nation's health-care ills fall rather neatly into four categories:

- Incremental/Free-Market
- Incremental/Social-Welfare

- Comprehensive/Free-Market
- Comprehensive/Social-Welfare

PLAN A: INCREMENTAL/FREE-MARKET

NAME: LIMITED MANAGED CARE
ADVOCATE: FORMER PRESIDENT BUSH
IDEA: TO OFFER TAX CREDITS AS INCENTIVE FOR
LOW-INCOME CONSUMERS TO SELECT THEIR OWN
HEALTH INSURANCE.
PRIMARY REFORMS:

Tax credits. Provides tax credits to low-income people to buy their own insurance (rather than having the government provide it directly).

HMO enrollment. Offers incentives to encourage people to enroll in health maintenance organizations (HMOs), which generally cut costs.

Insurance reform. Alters the private insurance market to help high-risk individuals get affordable insurance.

Cost caps. Places a cap on Medicare and Medicaid costs to pay for reforms.

Discussion: The key to this strategy is the increased use of HMOs. Backers of this option believe that HMOs and other prepaid insurance plans better scrutinize the treatment that doctors and hospitals offer (a debatable point).

PROS

- Introduces some market competition.
- Provides access to many Americans not now covered.
- Doesn't add to the burden of Medicare and Medicaid.
- Is relatively easy to implement.
- Could be easily expanded to include more comprehensive reforms.

CONS

- Leaves the unfair and inefficient employer-sponsored health-care system in place.
- Has no funding mechanism.
- Is contingent on capping Medicare and Medicaid costs—an unlikely prospect.
- Increases total health-care costs.

PLAN B: INCREMENTAL/SOCIAL-WELFARE _____

NAME: PAY OR PLAY
ADVOCATE: DEMOCRATIC CONGRESSIONAL
  LEADERSHIP
IDEA: TO ASSURE EVERY AMERICAN INSURANCE,
  EITHER THROUGH A PRIVATE PLAN OR THE
  GOVERNMENT.
PRIMARY REFORMS:

Payroll tax. Employers must either offer health insurance (paid jointly by employer and worker) or pay a payroll tax for health care.

AmeriCare. The tax finances AmeriCare, which provides coverage to anyone not covered by private plans.

Choice. Employers buy insurance from hundreds of private companies setting their own premiums. Patients may choose among doctors and hospitals setting their own prices.

No Medicaid. AmeriCare, which is administered by the states, replaces Medicaid.

Discussion: By relying on a payroll tax—and requiring that noncovered employed Americans buy into it—the plan would avoid some of Medicare's drawbacks. (Medicare has always depended on the political support of the general population, and has been severely underfinanced. It covers only 40 percent of the uninsured poor.)

PROS

- Provides universal coverage.
- Allows employed and insured Americans to keep their employer-sponsored insurance programs.
- Gives employers incentive to offer health plans.
- Forces employers to participate in the health-care system.
- Lets workers change jobs without fear of losing coverage.

CONS

- Creates a massive new bureaucracy.
- May lead to a two-tiered health-care system, dividing those insured by the government from those insured by employers.

- Is not designed to contain costs.
- Leaves the inefficient private health-care system in place.

PLAN C: COMPREHENSIVE/FREE-MARKET

NAME: CONSUMER CHOICE
ADVOCATE: THE HERITAGE FOUNDATION
IDEA: TO INCREASE COMPETITION AND INJECT COST-
CONSCIOUSNESS INTO HEALTH CARE BY FORCING
CONSUMERS TO COMPARISON-SHOP FOR INSURANCE
AND CARE.
PRIMARY REFORMS:

No employer tax breaks. Eliminates the tax exclusion employers now enjoy for providing health insurance (removing the incentive for companies to provide insurance).

Individual tax credits. Offers tax credits to individuals for health insurance or any health-related expenses (thus giving incentive to citizens to buy their own insurance).

Medicare and Medicaid. The poor, the elderly, and the unemployed continue to be covered through Medicare and Medicaid.

Credit based on income. Since the size of the tax credit is based on family income, the plan provides the most assistance to the poor and middle class.

Discussion: The plan blames our system's ills on the tax exemption now offered for employer-paid health insurance. Currently, the wealthy receive the biggest tax and benefit breaks—and consumers have little motivation to contain costs.

PROS

- Restores market principles to the selection of health insurance.
- Restores choice to individuals, requiring consumers to shop around for the best plan at the best price.
- Removes employers' burden to provide health care.
- Doesn't add new government bureaucracies.

CONS

- Doesn't address health-care needs of the uninsured underclass.
- Drastically increases the need for regulation of private insurance providers (increasing administrative red tape).
- Operates under the (untested) assumption that market competition will contain health-care costs.

PLAN D: COMPREHENSIVE/SOCIAL-WELFARE _____

NAME: UNIVERSAL COVERAGE
ADVOCATE: SEN. BOB KERREY
IDEA: TO REPLACE ALL OTHER HEALTH PROGRAMS
   WITH A NATIONAL HEALTH INSURANCE PLAN,
   FINANCED BY HIGHER TAXES.
PRIMARY REFORMS:

Health USA. The government establishes Health USA, a national health-care plan covering all citizens with a comprehensive package of services including preventive long-term care.

Health commission. A new National Health Commission administers the program and distributes money to state health programs.

Health-care tax. The program is paid for by a 5-percent payroll tax.

Elimination of other programs. Medicare, Medicaid, and all other government plans are scrapped.

Choice. Health care is still provided by private hospitals, physicians, and health professionals affiliated with private health plans, such as HMOs or managed-care programs.

PROS

- Provides unconditional access for all.
- Drastically cuts administrative expenses by eliminating the paperwork now generated by the wide variety of insurance companies, hospitals, and doctors.
- Controls health-care costs with built-in regulation mechanisms.
- Eliminates chance of financial ruin for families struck by costly catastrophic illness.

- Frees employers from the burdens of providing health care for employees.
- Overall, saves approximately $150 billion over five years, compared to current programs.

CONS

- Raises taxes significantly.
- Transfers $300 billion annually into the inefficient federal bureaucracy.
- Sets rigid limits on medical decisions and personal choice.
- May lead to long, difficult waiting periods for elective procedures.
- Removes incentives for physicians and hospitals to spend money on cutting-edge medical technology.
- May stifle medical research and innovation.

A NATIONAL REFERENDUM ON FOUR SOLUTIONS TO THE NATIONAL HEALTH-CARE CRISIS

THE PROBLEM

The American health-care system is broken. We spend far more on health care in both relative (12 percent of gross national product) and absolute terms ($738 billion) than any other developed nation. Yet 37 million Americans do not have insurance and another 30 million are underinsured. By objective standards, our health is slipping: we rank sixteenth in average life expectancy, and twenty-fifth in infant mortality. How can the system be reformed?

OPTION I: LIMITED MANAGED CARE

Provides tax credits to low-income people to buy their own private insurance, rather than having the government provide it directly. Offers incentives to encourage people to enroll in health maintenance organizations (HMOs) or other prepaid health systems, which are generally less costly. Reforms the private insurance market to help high-risk individuals obtain affordable insurance. Places a cap on Medicare and Medicaid costs to pay for program reforms.

OPTION II: PAY OR PLAY

Employers must either provide health insurance or pay a payroll tax to fund AmeriCare, which provides coverage to anyone not covered by private plans (including people now on Medicaid—which is eliminated by the plan—and the self-employed, and workers without company plans). Employers buy insurance from hundreds of private companies setting their own premiums. Citizens may choose among doctors and hospitals setting their own prices.

OPTION III: CONSUMER CHOICE

Eliminates the tax exclusion that employers now enjoy for providing health insurance—thus taking away the incentive for companies to provide insurance. Offers tax credits to individuals for health insurance or any health-related expenses—thus giving incentive to citizens to purchase their own insurance. The poor, the elderly, and the unemployed continue to be covered through Medicare and Medicaid. Since the size of the tax credit would be based on family income, the plan provides the most assistance to the poor and middle class.

OPTION IV: UNIVERSAL COVERAGE

The government establishes a national health-care plan—financed by a 5-percent payroll tax—covering all citizens with a comprehensive package of services, including preventive long-term care. The program is administered by a new National Health Commission, which distributes funds to state health programs. Medicare, Medicaid, and all other government plans are eliminated. Health care is still provided by private hospitals, physicians, and health professionals affiliated with private health plans.

☆   THE PEOPLE SPEAK...   ☆

ON HEALTH CARE

TOGETHER AND APART

We're united, yet we're divided.

When it comes to facing the health-care crisis, Americans share the fear and the concern. We're terrified by climbing costs, by the growing ranks of the uninsured, by the possibility of finding ourselves—or our children—sick with no way to pay for a doctor.

But that collective sense of fear hasn't drawn us together. It's split us in two:

- *The minimum.* A third of us favor the least sweeping plan.
- *The maximum.* Nearly as many favor the most comprehensive strategy.

The results show a unity of concern, and a divergence of resolve:

- **Plan A:** Limited Managed Care: 34 percent
- **Plan B:** Pay or Play: 13 percent
- **Plan C:** Consumer Choice: 20 percent
- **Plan D:** Universal Coverage: 29 percent

THE PARTY GAME

What influences Americans' opinions about the fate of health-care programs? Your choice of political party is one of the clearest indicators of where you're likely to stand on the issue:

DEMOCRATS

- 41 percent favor Universal Coverage.
- 18 percent favor Limited Managed Care.

REPUBLICANS

- 53 percent favor Limited Managed Care.
- 15 percent favor Universal Coverage.

WHAT'S IN IT FOR ME? _____

Those Americans who benefit most from the current state of health care are the most conservative in their preferences. And those who have the most to gain are the biggest supporters of large-scale reform.

INCOME

- *$50,000 or more:* 50 percent favor Limited Managed Care.
- *Less than $30,000:* 37 percent favor Universal Coverage.

AGE

- *18–29-year-olds:* 44 percent favor Universal Coverage.

RACE

- *Nonwhites:* 70 percent favor Universal Coverage.

FROM THE TOP

How does all of this fit in with the Clinton administration's efforts on health care? Certainly the issue hasn't been resolved. The President's strategy—which in its initial form would have been the most expensive social initiative since the New Deal—would be financed mainly through a new tax on cigarettes and savings on existing health-care programs. Would that be enough to cover the estimated $500 billion price tag over the first five years?[47]

Certainly, President Clinton's plan acknowledges the crisis and would guarantee that every American has at least minimal coverage, but it might place too large a burden on small businesses—or rely too much on the cigarette tax. It promises a lot without explaining where the money will come from.

More important, it's likely to be so watered down by the time it's passed that it will create more of a muddle than we started with. Things will change, but not enough to meet the challenges Americans have identified. Why? Clearly, what America needs on the health-care issue is leadership. And President Clinton hasn't demonstrated the leadership capacity to inspire people to follow him on such a massive policy overhaul. The problem with the Clinton plan, in other words, is President Clinton.

What will happen? The problems continue to fester, with special interests holding on to their preferences for dear life. Any change in health-care policy will take sacrifice. But that must start from the top. Until *all* Americans clearly understand what's at stake in the health-care crisis, there's no solution in sight.

CRIME

Amid the despair, we found hope.

Amid the fear, we found conviction.

Amid the violence, we found ideas.

We weren't surprised to find that crime is ravaging America. But we were astonished to find that Americans are prepared to fight it. And that they know how.

The Los Angeles riots showed that America is an instant away from anarchy. The People's Referendum on Crime shows that we're just as close to quashing the violence around us.

America is not a society of criminals. We're a society that has let the criminals get the upper hand. We feel unsafe in our own cities. In our own neighborhoods. In our own homes.

But Americans aren't cowering in fear. We're not giving up the streets.

We asked Americans: Have you given up hope?

And the answer, overwhelmingly, was: No.

When we asked people what to do about crime, we expected solutions born of trepidation—answers like locking our doors and flipping on our burglar alarms; building walls around our neighborhoods.

In place of anxiety, we got resolve. In place of resignation, we got plans—clear, rational, coordinated plans.

Because the people understand: we won't stop criminals with random, isolated measures. They told us that the way to halt crime ought to be through a coordinated vision—one that protects us and administers justice and brings safety. And restores hope.

We didn't get stopgap measures. Americans offered us a comprehensive approach to ridding ourselves of crime. They gave us an impressive plan to:

- *Empower the police,* giving law-enforcement officials the power to enforce the laws and restore safety.

- *Reform the courts,* ensuring that our judicial system administers justice fairly and that serious offenders aren't freed on technicalities.
- *Fix the prisons,* ensuring that our correctional facilities punish those who need punishment, and rehabilitate those who have hope of reform.
- *Control the weapons,* ridding the streets of the deadly guns that have caused countless deaths of innocent people.

Every minute. Everywhere.

Crime has come to affect nearly every American, nearly everywhere we go, nearly all the time. How often do violent crimes happen in America?[1]

- Murder: every twenty-two minutes
- Forcible rape: every five minutes
- Robbery: every forty-nine seconds
- Aggravated assault: every seventeen seconds

The specter of crime has not divided the nation. It hasn't torn us apart. And we're not ready to give up our streets. Rather, the crisis in our neighborhoods has forged a common resolve, a new sense of common purpose. It has united Americans in a war against a common enemy.

Crime stems from poverty, from social strife, from the innate violence of society. But mostly it arises from hopelessness. From the feeling that things won't get any better. And it feeds on itself: The less hope, the more crime. The more crime, the less hope.

Americans don't have a simple view of crime; they have a comprehensive view of the problem. They're ready to take action now. They're tired of waiting for the government to do something about the problem. And they're ready to send a unified message about what has to be done to save our neighborhoods from violence.

A MONSTER IN OUR MIDST

No one needs to be told that crime is ravaging our neighborhoods. It's everywhere. It's inescapable. On TV. In newspapers. On the street. What's shocking is this: However bad you think crime might be—it's probably worse. More violent. More pervasive. More extreme.

Crime is a perennial problem—one that will always be part of society. But two facts are striking:

- America has more crime now than ever before.
- America leads the world in crime.

OUT OF CONTROL

In the past three decades, crime has shot up in every major category, from theft to murder.

From 1960 to 1990, the number of crimes committed in the United States quadrupled—from 3.4 million to 14.5 million.[2]

The breakdown is startling:

- Aggravated assault shot up by six times.[3]
- Rape and robbery rose five times.[4]

In fact, in the five years from 1986 through 1990, crime in America rose by 10 percent—*and violent crime rose by 22 percent.*[5]

A SUPERPOWER OF VIOLENCE

Is crime simply the price we pay for living in a modern, industrial society? Maybe. But that doesn't explain the most striking fact of all about crime— that *America has more crime than any other nation.* In fact, three times as many Americans are killed every one hundred hours as were killed during the one-hundred hour Desert Storm ground assault.[6]

More killing. How does our murder rate compare to the rest of the world's?[7] The U.S. rate is:

- nine times Ireland's
- seven times Japan's
- four times Great Britain's

More rape. How does our frequency of rape compare to the rest of the world's?[8] The U.S. rate is:

- twenty-seven times Japan's
- five times Great Britain's
- four times Germany's

More gun murders. How many handgun-related murders took place in a single year?[9]

- Great Britain: 7
- Canada: 8
- United States: 8,915

MEAN STREETS

America has become the most violent society on earth. The brutality is everywhere—in cities and small towns, among the rich and the poor.

There is so much violence in America that it's overwhelming. Yet we can't face up to the problem of crime without defining it and understanding it. Americans know that before they solve a problem they have to look at the facts. So we took a look up close at the violent crime that has ravaged our nation.

What are the most common violent crimes?

- Aggravated assault
- Robbery
- Rape
- Murder

PROFILES IN CRIME

Here's a quick look at the four most common violent crimes:

Crime: Aggravated assault

Definition: Attacking for the purpose of inflicting serious injury

Annual incidents: 1,054,863[10]

Long-term increase: Up sixfold from 1960 to 1990[11]

Short-term increase: Up one quarter from 1987 to 1990[12]

Reports leading to arrest: 57 percent[13]

Perpetrators: 87 percent of those arrested are men.

Details: Occurs most often in the summer months.

Crime: Robbery

Definition: Taking anything by force or violence

Annual incidents: 639,271[14]

Long-term increase: Up fivefold from 1960 to 1990[15]

Short-term increase: Up 23 percent from 1987 to 1990[16]

Reports leading to arrest: 25 percent[17]

Perpetrators: 92 percent of those arrested are men, and 62 percent are under twenty-five years old.[18]

Details: Most common types of robbery are bank robbery (29 percent), street robbery (28 percent), convenience store robbery (24 percent).[19] How do robbers commit their crimes?[20]

- Strong-arm (brute force) tactics: 42 percent
- Firearms: 37 percent
- Knives: 12 percent

Crime: Forcible rape

Definition: Forcing a woman to have sex against her will

Annual incidents: 102,555[21]

Long-term increase: Up fivefold from 1960 to 1990[22]

Short-term increase: Up 12 percent from 1987 to 1990[23]

Reports leading to arrest: 53 percent[24]

Perpetrators: 44 percent of those arrested are under twenty-five; 43 percent are black.[25]

Details: Women are wary about reporting rape, and some experts estimate actual incidence could be ten times higher than official figures.

Crime: Murder

Definition: Willfully killing another person

Annual incidents: 23,438[26]

Long-term increase: Up 1.6 times from 1960 to 1990[27]

Short-term increase: Up 14 percent from 1987 to 1990[28]

Reports leading to arrest: 67 percent[29]

Perpetrators: 87 percent of those arrested are men.[30]

Details: Blacks are murder victims in extremely disproportionate numbers:

- 49 percent of murder victims in 1990 were black.[31]
- Murder is the leading cause of death for African-Americans aged fifteen to twenty-four.[32]
- The murder rate of young black men is up 90 percent since 1984.[33]

Firearms—used in nearly two-thirds of murders—are by far the most common weapons. And handguns are used in more than three in four firearm murders.[34] *The use of handguns in murders rose 47 percent from 1986 to 1990.*[35]

LIVING IN TERROR

Crime has changed our lives. It's terrified us. It's made us watch where we go—and when. Fear of crime has come to dictate where we choose to live, where we send our children to school, and where we work.

With the steadily increasing rates of violent crime, it's no wonder that most Americans live in constant fear for their lives and property.

Uneasy streets. Nearly two in five Americans say they feel uneasy on the streets.[36]

Afraid of the dark. How many Americans have areas within a mile of home where they're afraid to walk at night?[37]

- In 1967: 31 percent
- In 1992: 44 percent

Household safety. How many Americans feel unsafe in their own homes?[38]

- In 1990: 10 percent
- In 1992: 17 percent

As a result, Americans act out of fear. We've internalized the reality of crime so much that we live as if a criminal were lurking around every corner.

Changing our lives. How many Americans say fear of crime has made them[39]

- Purchase a weapon: 18 percent
- Limit the places or times they'll work: 22 percent
- Limit the places or times they'll shop: 32 percent
- Limit the places they'll go by themselves: 60 percent

THE BIG QUESTION: WHY?

Crime is nothing new. And there always will be crime. Violence, theft, and murder date from prehistoric times. But there's more crime now than ever before. And America leads the world. Why?

Before we could launch our search for solutions to the crime problem, we had to look for explanations. Why is there so much crime? Why is it increasing so steadily, and so much?

We found four factors that help explain the sharp increases:

- Drug use
- Delinquency among the young
- Factors of race
- A culture of violence

THE ENEMY WITHIN: DRUGS

Throughout the culture of crime, the impact of increased drug use has been felt.

1. *More drug crimes.* The proportion of jail inmates charged with drug offenses tripled between 1983 and 1989.[40]

- More than a quarter of all jail prisoners have committed drug crimes.

2. *More crime to obtain drug money.* What percentage of jail inmates say they committed their offense in order to get money to buy drugs?[41]

   - Murder: 2.8 percent
   - Larceny/theft: 27.8 percent
   - Robbery: 32.4 percent

3. *More criminals with drug histories.* What percentage of jail inmates say they have a history of drug use?[42]

   - 18–24-year-olds: 80 percent
   - 25–29-year-olds: 84 percent
   - 30–34-year-olds: 82 percent

4. *Drug use during criminal offenses.* What percentage of criminals were under the influence of drugs at the time of their offense?[43]

   - Murder: 6 percent
   - Robbery: 18 percent
   - Burglary: 20 percent

TEENAGE WASTELAND: YOUTH AND CRIME

Crime watchers have found a consistent pattern: the more young males in the population, the higher the crime rates. Young men account for a shockingly high proportion of American crime. *Fifty-six percent of all people arrested are between sixteen and twenty-nine years old.*[44]

Crime and the young. How many people charged with crimes are under twenty-five years old?[45]

- Assault: 41 percent
- Rape: 44 percent
- Murder: 49 percent
- Auto theft: 73 percent

Youthful indiscretions. How many high school seniors have taken part in delinquent activities?[46]

- Purposefully damaged school property: 13 percent
- Gotten into trouble with police: 23 percent
- Shoplifted: 31 percent
- Stolen something worth under fifty dollars: 32 percent

COLOR WARS: THE RACE FACTOR

A shockingly high number of African-Americans are arrested for violent crimes.

Disproportionate numbers. What percentage of those arrested are black?[47]

- Rape: 43 percent
- Murder: 56 percent
- Robbery: 65 percent

Blacks as victims. How many black crime victims are there for every one white victim?[48]

- Aggravated assault: 1.5
- Rape: 2
- Robbery: 2.4

In 1988, blacks accounted for 38 percent of the American prison population.[49]

AT THE MOVIES: VIOLENCE IN CULTURE

Crime and violence are so present that they're invisible. Murder is so prevalent that we've become callous to the disastrous situation of our cities and neighborhoods.

Movies. The murder rate is skyrocketing even on the silver screen. How many deaths per movie?

- *RoboCop* (1987): 32
- *RoboCop II* (1990): 82

- *Die Hard* (1989): 18
- *Die Hard 2* (1991): 264

Television. The National Coalition on Television estimates that by the age of eighteen, the average American has witnessed two hundred thousand violent acts on television—including forty thousand murders.

THE BIG OVERHAUL: CHANGING THE SYSTEM

We can't combat America's crime problem with isolated measures. To be effective, the nation needs a comprehensive approach to the crisis. We need to fight the war on all fronts.

Arenas of change. Once we had a full understanding of the complexity and the extent of the crime problem, we considered the many paths to solving the problem. We sought effective, innovative ways to ensure that

- Police can combat criminals on the streets.
- Our courts administer justice.
- Our prisons punish and reform.

Big questions. Further, we sought the answers to two pressing questions facing American society:

- Is capital punishment an effective deterrent to crime?
- How can we banish the scourge of handgun violence?

POLICE: THE FIRST FRONT

How effective are our police? Of the three sectors of the American criminal justice system—police, courts, and prisons—the nation's police force is the most effective, and the one for which Americans voice the least disfavor.

Public approval. What percentage of Americans said these sectors were "only fair" or "poor"?[50]

- Prisons: 54 percent
- Judges: 48 percent
- Police: 34 percent

In fact, the nation's police have shown increasing effectiveness, apprehending suspects with greater and greater frequency.

Crime fighting. Of every 100 reported crimes, how many led to an
arrest?[51]

- In 1980: 19.2
- In 1990: 21.6

(Only about 10 percent of felony arrests lead to conviction, and 2 percent
to actual jail time.[52])

Still, the nation's police force faces problems of ineffectiveness. There
are four main problems:

- There aren't enough officers.
- Police spend too much energy on work besides crime-fighting.
- Police lack power and authority in some vital law-enforcement
  areas.
- Old methods of policing have proven ineffective.

These are the challenges. And every challenge needs a response.
We've come up with innovations aimed at making the nation's crime-
fighting forces stronger and more effective.

1. SHOULD WE HAVE MORE POLICE OFFICERS? _____

The crime rate has grown, but the police force has stayed the same size.
While crime has increased greatly in recent decades, the number of police officers per capita hasn't increased. We've had about 2.4 police officers for every 1,000 Americans since the mid-1970s.[53]

Many experts and government officials have suggested increasing the
nation's police force by about 20 percent—by 100,000 officers.

The cost. What would law enforcement cost the average family of four
in taxes?[54]

- Now: $456 annually
- With increase: $556 annually

The benefit. How would the increase affect the ratio of police in the
population?

- Now: 2.4 officers per 1,000 people
- With increase: 2.9 officers per 1,000 people

The increase would mean about three million more arrests annually.

2. SHOULD WE GIVE POLICE MORE TIME TO FIGHT CRIME?

What do police officers do with their time? Less than a third of their activities involve actually fighting crime.[55] In fact, twelve out of one hundred police officers spend all their time on desk duties. We need police who fight crime in the streets, not from behind desks.

3. SHOULD WE GIVE THE POLICE MORE POWER?

How much power should police officers have? The U.S. Constitution protects the rights of citizens accused of crimes by limiting the actions police may take in enforcing the law. Two fundamental issues are worth reconsidering:

- Under what conditions may police stop and question a suspect?
- How much force should police officers be able to use in apprehending suspects?

Probable cause. The Constitution stipulates that an officer must have "probable cause" to stop and question a citizen. This protects individual rights, but it restricts officers' ability to fight crime effectively. It's a trade-off: Should we sacrifice a constitutional guarantee for the benefit of enforcing the law more strictly?

Using force. Police may use deadly force only when they or others are threatened with serious harm. But recent years have brought countless incidents in which the public has questioned officers' use of force in apprehending or pursuing suspects.

Americans have observed a sharp increase in police brutality in the past three decades. How many Americans believe there is police brutality where they live?[56]

- 1965: 9 percent
- 1991: 35 percent

Still, with ever-rising rates of violent crime, police say they need to be clear about their rights and powers in fighting crime. The 1992 Rodney King case in Los Angeles—and the riots that followed—made clear that police use of force is among the most sensitive and explosive issues the nation faces. A consensus must be reached, and terms must be carefully defined.

4. SHOULD POLICE UPGRADE THEIR METHODS? _____

In America, a police officer's job is to react. Police are alerted to crimes, and they get to work. But should the nation's crime-fighting forces take a more *active* role? Should they incorporate new methods to fight the ever-increasing rate of crime?

Problems, not incidents. The National Institute of Justice has called for a more comprehensive, holistic approach to fighting crime, labeled "Problem-Oriented Policing."

Community policing. Another view advocates making police officers integral parts of communities—not outsiders brought in to deal with isolated incidents. Under this approach community residents take active roles in working with police officers. And officers are permanently assigned to specific neighborhoods. Finally, this approach dictates that police get out of their squad cars and onto their feet. Foot patrols enhance contact between citizens and police, and give officers greater understanding of neighborhoods.[57]

THE COURTS: RESTORING JUSTICE

Is the nation's judicial system doing its job?

Americans don't think so. More than eight in ten Americans say their local courts don't deal harshly enough with criminals.

The problems:

- Criminals are getting off too easily.
- Technicalities of the law make it difficult to make convictions.
- Even when convicted, many criminals don't end up serving the sentences they deserve.

Issues to consider:

- *Pretrial detention.* Measures to keep suspects off the streets.
- *Plea bargaining.* Guilty pleas in exchange for lighter sentences.
- *Exclusionary rule.* Keeping inadmissible evidence out of the court-room.
- *Sentencing.* Should it be more rigid?

1. SHOULD COURTS WORK TO KEEP SUSPECTS BEHIND BARS—EVEN BEFORE THEY'VE BEEN CONVICTED?

More and more, courts are posting exceedingly high bails—or denying bail altogether—as methods of keeping criminal suspects in detention before their trials. But this presents a legal and moral quandary: Do Americans want their courts to use their discretion in deciding who will be free—and who won't—before justice has run its course? Is public safety more important than individual rights?

2. SHOULD PLEA BARGAINING BE CURBED TO REQUIRE STRICTER SENTENCES FOR CRIMINALS?

The court system in which every suspect actually undergoes a trial is a thing of the past. Why? The judicial system is so overwhelmed with cases that, without plea bargaining, it would become overloaded and come to a grinding halt.

How widespread is plea bargaining? The facts:

- Felony convictions stemming from guilty pleas: 96 percent
- Felony convictions stemming from trials: 4 percent

The result: Plea bargaining makes a mockery of the justice system.

- Few people are tried for the crimes they committed.
- The poor and powerless are often forced to plead guilty to crimes they didn't commit.

Is there a way to eliminate plea bargaining? Only by expanding the court system. At the minimum, the nation would have to double—or triple—the system's capacity to try cases. And it would cost billions. The question: Is the money better spent putting police on the streets, or judges on the bench?

3. SHOULD WE ALLOW ILLEGALLY OBTAINED EVIDENCE IN COURT? _____

Every year, hundreds of criminals go free—even when there is compelling evidence of their guilt. Why? Because the key evidence against them has been gathered in an illegal manner. The so-called "exclusionary rule" forbids its use in court. It comes down to a question of whose rights are more important: the accused's, or the victim's.

4. SHOULD WE BE STRICTER ABOUT PUNISHING CRIMINALS? _____

By and large, crime goes unpunished in America. A criminal committing a felony has a 1-in-100 chance of being convicted and serving jail time. The punishments meted out to that tiny minority are getting more and more lenient.

What was the average jail term for robbery?[58]

- In 1896: 56 months
- In 1988: 38 months

Most convicted criminals today receive "indeterminate" sentences—jail time that's at the discretion of judges or parole boards. And very few prisoners serve the time to which they were sentenced. *Only thirteen in one hundred prisoners serve their full sentences.*[59] The rest are let out on parole, receive probation, or other early releases.

Does that mean they won't repeat their offenses? No. About one-third of those released early end up back in prison for violating the terms of their releases.[60]

What can be done to ensure that criminals get the sentences they deserve—and that they're not let out too early?

- Raise the minimum prison time required before release.
- Establish "determinate" sentences that dictate specific sentences for specific crimes.[61]

PRISONS: REFORMING THE REFORMATORIES

What is the purpose of prison?

We have the world's largest prison system. Yet we don't have a coherent idea of what purpose prison serves.

How many Americans are behind bars? In the 1980s, the prison population doubled—to 1.1 million inmates.[62] Another 3 million criminals are on probation or parole.

That growth brought a severe financial toll: state spending on prison construction in the eighties grew four times faster than education spending.[63]

But we're still unclear about the purpose of prison. Without a coherent philosophy, the nation can't make priorities in deciding the future of the penal system.

What purpose does prison serve? Four points of view prevail:

- *To punish.* Penalizing criminals for their actions.
- *To incapacitate.* Making criminals incapable of repeating their offenses.
- *To deter.* Preventing criminals—and others—from committing similar crimes in the future.
- *To rehabilitate.* To change criminals for the better through proper treatment.

We need definitive answers. If our objective is merely to get criminals off the streets, then the priority is to build more prison cells. If our goal is to reform criminals, then we ought to put money into educational, counseling, and vocational training programs. Prison must change to meet the demands of America.

CAPITAL PUNISHMENT: WHO DESERVES DEATH?

Should we kill our killers? As the nation continues to debate ways to punish criminals and prevent crime, the death penalty remains one of the most controversial and divisive elements of criminal justice.

Since the 1960s, support has been growing for punishing our criminals with death. How many Americans support capital punishment?[64]

- In 1966: 42 percent
- In 1991: 76 percent

Why the strong support? Those who back the death penalty are divided in their motivations:

- Revenge: 42 percent
- It deters crime: 35 percent
- Jails don't rehabilitate: 22 percent
- Criminals get off too easy today: 14 percent

Consensus on the death penalty is impossible, of course, because the issue touches on so many conflicting moral and religious convictions.

Racial bias. Among the primary arguments against the death penalty is that it tends to be enforced unequally. What were the races of those executed in the United States between 1930 and 1992?[65]

- Black: 53 percent
- White: 46 percent
- Other: 1 percent

A brutal society. Supporters argue that there is no surer way of getting murderers off the streets than capital punishment. Yet opponents maintain that it's not worth the price it exacts on society.

GUN CONTROL: DISARMING NUMBERS

Guns are inescapable in America. They are everywhere. Four in ten Americans say they have a gun in their homes.[66] There are two hundred million firearms in circulation in America.[67] Most of them aren't registered. Police estimate that there are two million guns in New York City. How many are registered? Just fifty thousand.[68]

Guns are used in 64 percent of American murders.[69]

As crime rises, what to do about guns remains a divisive issue, with two strong positions:

- Guns are the source of death and destruction.
- Guns are our first line of defense against crime.

How many Americans favor an all-out ban on handgun possession (except by police and other authorized people)?[70]

- In 1980: 31 percent
- In 1991: 43 percent

Despite the shift those numbers indicate, more than half of Americans still oppose a ban.[71]

But there is much stronger support for less stringent measures to control guns in society. How many Americans favor requiring police permits in order to purchase guns?[72]

- In 1980: 69 percent
- In 1991: 81 percent

The most popular gun-control measure of all is the idea—promoted by James Brady, President Reagan's press secretary—of requiring a seven-day waiting period before a handgun can be purchased. The idea of a seven-day wait has the support of 91 percent of Americans.[73] Finally, in late 1993, the Brady Bill received the support of Congress and became law.

THE PEOPLE'S CRIME BILL: A NATIONAL REFERENDUM

Crime is spiraling out of control. The $60 billion we throw at it annually isn't paying off; the half-million police officers—and one million security officers—seem inadequate; the incarceration of more than 1.1 million criminals doesn't make a dent.

Crime isn't an isolated issue—it's rooted in all of society's problems: poverty, drug addiction, gangs. Still, in solving the crime crisis, there's a need to focus on specific, concrete steps to address directly the problems at hand. The people's crime agenda focuses on three areas: the police, the judicial system, and the prison system.

Many of these proposals come with built-in costs—either financial or constitutional:

- *Financial.* These measures would require increases in local, state, and federal taxes.
- *Constitutional.* These measures would risk narrowing the legal rights of Americans—specifically, criminal suspects and convicts.

Are the innovations worth the costs? Is public safety worth the price paid in civil liberty? That's the question Americans must answer.

POLICE REFORM

1. *More police.* Increase the nation's police force by 20 percent. Estimated cost: $100 per household.

    Favor [   ]   Oppose [   ]

2. *Stopping suspects.* Give police greater discretion to stop, question, search, and detain possible suspects—based on the officers' judgment, but without probable cause.

    Favor [   ]   Oppose [   ]

3. *Using force.* Give police greater discretion in determining when and how much force (including deadly force) is appropriate to apprehend suspects or intercede at the scene of a crime.

    Favor [   ]   Oppose [   ]

4. *Neighborhood participation.* Create local community and neighborhood patrols staffed by concerned citizens who patrol the neighborhood and report problems to the police.

Favor [   ]   Oppose [   ]

5. *Community policing.* Enact community policing:

- Put police on foot patrols.
- Have police work more closely with families and troubled children before they become criminals.
- Take these measures even at the risk of having fewer officers available for more traditional police duties.

Favor [   ]   Oppose [   ]

6. *"Military" deployment.* Deploy police en masse to target crime hot spots, using almost military techniques to maintain law and order.

Favor [   ]   Oppose [   ]

COURT REFORM

7. *Expanded courts.* Expand local, state, and federal court systems to help try (and convict) a greater proportion of criminal offenders. Estimated cost: $100 annually per household.

Favor [   ]   Oppose [   ]

8. *Plea-bargain ban.* Curtail—or eliminate—plea bargaining for violent offenses, requiring individuals to stand trial for—or

plead guilty to—the crimes for which they are originally charged.

Favor [   ]   Oppose [   ]

9. *Fixed sentences.* Require convicted criminals to serve fixed sentences for specific crimes, rather than allowing judges a wide range in setting sentences.

Favor [   ]   Oppose [   ]

10. *Minimum sentences.* Establish higher minimum sentences— that *must* be imposed and served—for all those convicted of violent crimes.

Favor [   ]   Oppose [   ]

11. *Full sentences.* Require all those convicted of violent crimes to serve their full sentences—and drastically curtail the use of parole, probation, and other conditional releases.

Favor [   ]   Oppose [   ]

12. *Pretrial detention.* Grant judges greater discretion in keeping violent-crime suspects off the streets before their trials—by using high bails or denying bail altogether.

Favor [   ]   Oppose [   ]

13. *Relevant evidence.* Loosen the "exclusionary rule," so that all relevant evidence—regardless of how it was obtained—can be admissible in criminal trials.

Favor [   ]   Oppose [   ]

PRISON REFORM _____

14. *More prisons.* Build more prisons so that more criminals can be sent to prison and current prisoners can be incarcerated longer. Estimated cost: $100 annually per household.

Favor [ ]   Oppose [ ]

15. *Alternative programs.* Expand alternatives to prison for criminals who don't pose an immediate threat to society—such as boot camps, house arrest, community service, and mandatory drug treatment.

Favor [ ]   Oppose [ ]

GUN CONTROL _____

16. *Constitutional change.* Pass a constitutional amendment repealing the Second Amendment right "to keep and bear arms."

Favor [ ]   Oppose [ ]

17. *Licensing and waiting.* Institute strict licensing and waiting periods prior to gun purchases.

Favor [ ]   Oppose [ ]

18. *Assault-weapons ban.* Ban the sale or possession of all assault weapons.

Favor [ ]   Oppose [ ]

19. *Prison for possession.* Enact a mandatory prison sentence of one or more years for anyone illegally in possession of a gun.

Favor [ ]   Oppose [ ]

20. *Civil liability.* Make gun manufacturers and/or licensing authorities legally responsible, and thus liable for civil damage
suits, for the violence and damage caused by the guns they
help place in circulation.

Favor [ ]   Oppose [ ]

CAPITAL PUNISHMENT

21. *Death penalty.* Keep and expand the use of capital punishment.

Favor [ ]   Oppose [ ]

22. *Use of the penalty.* The death penalty should be given for each
of the following offenses:

First-degree murder	Favor [ ]	Oppose [ ]
Killing a police officer	Favor [ ]	Oppose [ ]
Committing murder during a felony	Favor [ ]	Oppose [ ]
Running a child prostitution ring	Favor [ ]	Oppose [ ]
Selling drugs to children	Favor [ ]	Oppose [ ]
Committing serial murders	Favor [ ]	Oppose [ ]
Committing acts of terror	Favor [ ]	Oppose [ ]
Rape	Favor [ ]	Oppose [ ]
Spying for the Russians	Favor [ ]	Oppose [ ]
Industrial spying for the Japanese	Favor [ ]	Oppose [ ]
Killing accidentally while driving drunk	Favor [ ]	Oppose [ ]

23. *Death row limits.* Set limits on legal appeals for inmates on
death row—so that years, or even decades, don't pass between sentencing and execution.

Favor [ ]   Oppose [ ]

THE PEOPLE SPEAK... ☆

ON CRIME

☆

What has led to America's frightening crime rate? The roots of the problem may lie in history, economics, sociology, and racial issues. These matters are central, but their scope is vast. For this section, we put crime under a microscope, and take on factors with direct links to crime: the police, the courts, and the prisons.

THE POLICE

1. MORE POLICE: NO
Americans don't feel a shortage of police officers—at least, not enough to want to pay the salaries for more.

- Would you pay $100 annually to expand the local police force by 20 percent? Only *38 percent* said yes.

2. MORE POWER FOR POLICE: YES
Trading rights for safety. The fear is rampant. Americans are so afraid of crime that the situation has reached a shocking point: most Americans are willing to sacrifice their very constitutional rights in order to have safer streets.

In large numbers, Americans want police to be able to enforce the law *with authority.*

- *85 percent* support giving police greater discretion in deciding when to use force—including deadly force—in apprehending suspects at the scene of a crime.
- *54 percent* favor giving police more discretion in stopping and questioning suspects—*even without probable cause to do so.*

163

3. CITIZEN PATROLS: YES

In addition to giving more power to their police, Americans are increasingly willing to take matters into their own hands.

- *75 percent* say they would help to form and support local community and neighborhood patrols to be staffed by citizens patrolling their own neighborhoods.

4. INNOVATIVE POLICING: YES

Police can have more impact on crime simply by employing novel methods of crime fighting. They can do more than simply respond to crimes: they can prevent them.

Community policing. Chief Willie Williams, of the Los Angeles Police Department, has been an active advocate of community policing: police patrol by foot and work with neighborhood families and merchants; they take an active role in the community, rather than simply responding when crimes occur.

- *85 percent* of Americans express support for community policing programs as crime-fighting measures.

Mass deployment. The flip side of community policing is responding to crime in almost military fashion, deploying police en masse to crime hot spots, overwhelming and intimidating the perpetrators of crimes.

- *48 percent* of Americans supported mass deployments to fight crime.

THE COURTS _____

1. KEEPING SUSPECTS BEHIND BARS: YES

Innocent until proven guilty? That central tenet of the Constitution is, in many ways, the backbone of the nation's criminal justice system. Yet the violent state of the nation has led to a newer sentiment: If people might be dangerous, Americans want them behind bars.

- *80 percent* of Americans want to give judges discretion to keep violent-crime suspects in jail—with high bail or no bail option—before their trials begin.

Why do so many of us want to take away the rights of criminal suspects? The answer is simple: fear. Why? In a name, Willie Horton. Too often, we read and hear stories of suspects committing horrific crimes while free on bail. Which is more important: the rights of a suspect, or the right of ordinary citizens not to be attacked, raped, or murdered? The people have made their opinion clear.

2. CURB PLEA BARGAINING AND EXPAND THE COURTS: YES

Consider two points.

- In almost every U.S. criminal case, suspects never stand trial for the crimes they are accused of committing.
- Most criminals are convicted of crimes less serious than those they were originally charged with.

Why? Plea bargaining. Americans are fed up with a system that doesn't punish criminals for their crimes.

- *87 percent* of Americans want to curtail—or even eliminate—plea bargaining for violent crimes.

The direct result of that change would certainly be more and longer criminal trials. But Americans are willing to put up with that prospect— and to foot the bill.

- *94 percent* of Americans would pay $100 more in taxes annually to expand the local, state, and federal courts to allow for more trials and convictions of criminals.

3. LOOSEN THE EXCLUSIONARY RULE: YES

How scared are we? Americans want so badly to put criminals behind bars that they're willing to sacrifice constitutional rights if it will help make the streets safer. That's how deep the fear is.

- *58 percent* of Americans would be willing to loosen the laws restricting the use of improperly obtained evidence in criminal trials.

The bottom line: We just don't want to see criminals get off on technicalities, no matter what the cost. Most Americans would allow all relevant evidence—no matter how it was obtained—to be brought into a criminal trial.

4. BE STRICTER IN PUNISHING CRIMINALS: YES

In short, Americans want to put muscle back into their criminal justice system. They're sick of the hypocrisy. They're sick of seeing criminals out on the streets. They're sick of criminals knowing they can get away with just about anything and not be punished.

Mandatory sentences. Ninety-eight percent of Americans say anyone convicted of a crime should serve the full sentence—without parole or probation.

Preset terms. Ninety-seven percent say the sentences should be preset for each crime—not left to the discretion of the judge.

Minimum sentences. Ninety-six percent want to impose higher minimum sentences—for all criminal convicts.

PRISON REFORM _____

To have teeth in the law, there must be consequences for crimes. Issuing harsher sentences doesn't mean anything if there's nowhere to put the criminals behind bars.

It's not surprising, considering the rampant fear of crime, that Americans are united in their attitudes about prison: they want criminals to go to prison and stay there.

1. MORE PRISONS: YES

When criminals are convicted, we need places to put them—and to keep them.

- *84 percent* of Americans would pay higher taxes and support measures in their states to build more prisons.

2. ALTERNATIVES TO PRISON: NO

Americans don't seem to care about the effectiveness or long-term benefits of alternatives to prison, such as "house arrest" and "boot camps." It's simple: they want their criminals behind bars.

- *21 percent* of Americans advocate alternatives to prison.

CAPITAL PUNISHMENT

An eye for an eye. A tooth for a tooth. A life for a life.

Capital punishment is the most instinctive, gut-level response of Americans to the fear of crime. Some have called it cruel, repulsive, severe, dehumanizing.

In our research, Americans sent a clear message. They want the death penalty, and they want it now.

- *92 percent* support the death penalty.
- *93 percent* support setting limits on legal appeals for death-row inmates—so sentences can be carried out without years and decades of delay.

What sorts of crimes should be punishable by death? Americans are fairly united in their desire to use this most severe punishment for a wide range of offenses:

- Serial murder: 92 percent
- Killing a police officer: 91 percent
- Terrorism: 84 percent
- Murder during a felony: 82 percent
- Prostituting children: 64 percent
- Rape: 54 percent

DRUGS

What if drugs were legal? What if you could walk into any supermarket and pick up a bag of marijuana—the way you might purchase, say, a six-pack of beer?

In facing the nation's growing drug crisis, Americans have only three choices:

- To make drugs legal
- To crack down severely on users and dealers
- To educate Americans and prevent drug use

One option is not available: to do nothing.

Why is inaction an unacceptable choice? It's simple: because drug use is destroying America. As we'll show in this chapter, drug abuse isn't an isolated menace affecting only certain ethnic groups or certain neighborhoods or certain age groups.

It's everywhere. It plagues people of all ages, of all backgrounds. It affects those who use drugs, and those who don't. It affects us at work and at home.

It's inescapable.

Aren't all antidrug efforts important? Certainly. But the crisis is so pressing—and the resources so limited—that it's time to make choices. To set priorities. That's what the people told us. If we had the money—and the resolve—we could pour billions of dollars into tough law enforcement, while simultaneously pumping billions more into the effort to teach people about drugs and rehabilitate those who are already addicted. We could expend unlimited efforts to fight the scourge on every front.

Americans don't need to be told what the problem is; they need to decide how to solve it.

It's time to choose our approach. And Americans told us with conviction which approach they favor. They said without question that it's time to get to work. And they told us that when it comes to drugs, the status quo won't do. Something must be done.

THE TIME IS NOW

We don't have a choice. Drugs have become such a blight on American society that we must take determined action; if we sit by and watch, the plague will destroy America.

Four pressing factors make the issue urgent:

- Crack alone is ravaging countless lives.
- Intravenous drug use is spreading AIDS.
- Drug crime has turned cities into killing fields.
- The cost is draining government and business.

CRACK: CHEAP AND DEADLY

Since it was introduced in the mid-1980s, crack has become the drug of choice on inner-city streets. Why? It's cheap (three dollars per dose); it acts instantly and with intensity; and it's easy to use (it's smoked in a pipe). Nearly three million Americans have used crack.

Health. Crack has become the leading cause of drug-related emergency room visits in the nation's biggest cities.[1] How many people were admitted to emergency rooms for crack-related cases?[2]

- In 1984: 549
- In 1988: 15,306

Babies. Many women have chosen to use crack as an alternative to intravenous drugs. As a result, more than 100,000 babies are prenatally exposed to cocaine or crack each year.[3] The cost to taxpayers? More than $20 billion a year.

Crime. While drugs like marijuana and heroin suppress the central nervous system and aren't conducive to committing crimes, crack users are likely to commit violent and illegal acts while under the influence of the drug. How many of those arrested in big cities test positive for crack or cocaine? Up to 60 percent.[4]

AIDS: THE IV PLAGUE

Drug use has contributed to the tragic AIDS epidemic in two significant ways:

- *IV needles.* Sharing of intravenous needles directly transmits the disease.
- *Sexual activity.* Crack use often leads to increased sexual activity— and the trading of sex for drugs.

How many cases of full-blown AIDS are caused by IV drug use alone? Twenty-one percent.

Who pays the price? Not just the users. It is estimated that up to half of the babies born to HIV-infected mothers will go on to develop full-blown AIDS.

CRIME: A CYCLE OF VIOLENCE

It's a vicious picture: Addicts commit crimes to get drugs. And drugs make criminals commit more crimes. The more drugs, the more crime— the more serious.

How do we know? Drug tests prove it.

- How many of those arrested have used drugs in the thirty-six hours prior to their arrests?
  - Nationally: 56 percent[5]
- How many men arrested test positive for drugs?[6]
  - In Los Angeles: 69 percent
  - In Chicago: 73 percent
  - In New York: 79 percent

What impact does drug use have on criminals? It's indisputable that when drug users are on drugs, they commit more crime, and when they're off drugs, they commit less crime.[7] How much of an effect do drugs have?

- Criminals are up to six times more active when they are on drugs than when they aren't.[8]

THE COST: DRAINING OUR RESOURCES _____

The financial toll drugs take on America is astronomical. Consider just three areas:

- The cost of law enforcement
- The cost of drug crimes
- The cost to businesses caused by drug-addicted employees

Law enforcement. In 1992, the federal government spent $11.9 billion on antidrug programs. Adding the cost of state and local police, and court and prisons measures related to drugs, the national total comes to about $28 billion.

Theft and burglary. Drug addicts often steal to support their habits. It's estimated that about $8 billion is taken each year in drug-related crimes.

Business losses. Employees who use drugs are likely to miss work, injure themselves on the job, and file for worker's compensation. In all, drug abuse costs employers $100 billion annually—about $7,621 per abusing employee.[9]

Finally, drugs shatter families. And the government puts billions of dollars into public-assistance programs to support them.

A HOLLOW VICTORY

Ironically, we're winning the war on drugs. The casual use of drugs is down in many sectors of American society.

Overall. How many Americans used drugs regularly?[10]

- In 1985: 23 million
- In 1988: 14.5 million

Cocaine users. How many Americans used cocaine?[11]

- In 1985: 5.8 million
- In 1989: 2.9 million

Teens. How many high school students used drugs regularly?[12]

- In 1978: one in nine
- In 1988: one in thirty-three

In fact, drug use among teenagers has dropped sharply. Between 1980 and 1991, among high school seniors:[13]

- Marijuana use dropped 39 percent.
- Cocaine use dropped 50 percent.
- PCP use dropped 60 percent.

So why all the alarm? Because the number of *heavy abusers* is up—and because the most popular drugs are getting stronger and more devastating. Crack, specifically, is destroying our cities.

THE WAY OUT: EXPLORING THE SOLUTIONS

In considering how to solve the drug crisis, we investigated three options: making drugs legal, toughening law enforcement, or putting more effort into education and rehabilitation. The case for each is compelling.

THE END OF PROHIBITION: EXPLORING LEGALIZATION

THE IDEA
Laws against drugs may do more harm than good. We may need an entirely new approach. In a single stroke, making drugs legal would

- Eliminate the black market for drugs.
- Slash crime caused by addicts trying to get money to buy expensive illegal drugs.
- Curtail medical problems caused by the illegal nature of the drug market, not drugs themselves.

THE DETAILS
The simplest approach to legalization is basic: Make all drugs legal. But the most common strategy stops shy of that broad stroke. It would put

currently illegal drugs in the same regulated category as alcohol and tobacco.

- *Regulation.* Drugs such as marijuana, cocaine, and heroin would be strictly regulated and sold in specially licensed stores.
- *Minors.* Sales to minors would not be permitted.
- *Labels.* Products would carry warning labels like those on cigarettes and alcohol.
- *Advertising.* Drug advertising would be strictly controlled or banned.
- *Driving.* Driving under the influence would be illegal—and additional penalties would be instituted for committing other crimes while on drugs.

THE FRAMEWORK

Legalization is based on three ideas:

- *Individual rights.* A citizen has the right to take part in any activity as long as it does not directly infringe on the rights and freedom of others.
- *Counterproductivity.* Most of the "costs" of the drug problem stem from the very strategy meant to cure the problem—regulation.
- *Cost-effectiveness.* Antidrug laws and law enforcement simply aren't worth their financial expense.

THE ARGUMENT

1. *Individual liberty.* In a free society, the state does not have the right to dictate to its citizens what substances they can or cannot put into their bodies. (The state may, however, hold the individual responsible for the reckless consequences of using substances.)
2. *Police abuse.* Since drug abuse is a victimless crime without a "complaining" party, police must resort to intrusive, constitutionally dubious tactics to seek out illicit behavior. The result is an excessive use of unjustified searches, entrapment, and electronic surveillance.
3. *Alcohol and tobacco.* Drug use is no more or less immoral, unhealthy, or dangerous than the use of alcohol and tobacco, which are currently legal.

4. *Government control.* Combining legalization with thoughtful regulation would be a healthy way of monitoring what is now a dangerous, uncontrolled area. By restricting advertising, and issuing regulations like those currently limiting the sale and use of alcohol, the government could keep drug use under control.

5. *Black market.* Making drugs legal would eliminate the black market—the source of the most virulently damaging aspects of the illegal nature of drugs. At least half of the violent crime in major U.S. cities is committed by sellers and buyers as a result of drug prohibition.[14]

    Black market prices of heroin and cocaine are about one hundred times greater than their pharmaceutical prices. Drugs are expensive—and users often commit crimes to pay for habits that would be affordable if drugs were legal.

6. *The failure of interdiction.* In recent years, drug-enforcement efforts—specifically international interdiction—have increased dramatically. But the drug market has barely been affected: drugs today are cheaper and more widely available than ever. Why?

    • *Ineffectiveness.* Interdiction efforts prevent only about one in one hundred kilograms of cocaine from entering the United States.[15]

    • *Many sources.* Wherever drug-eradication efforts succeed, other regions and countries are quick to fill the void.

    • *Huge quantities.* It takes only a small proportion of the cultivated marijuana, opium, and cocaine to satisfy American demand.

7. *Stronger, deadlier.* An unintended effect of laws against drugs is that drugs on the market become ever stronger and deadlier. The stronger the laws, the more potent the drugs: crack, PCP, ice, and other drugs keep getting stronger.

    In contrast, legalized drugs are getting weaker: tobacco companies are marketing low-tar cigarettes; brewers sell light and nonalcoholic beer; wine makers sell wine coolers.

8. *AIDS.* One-quarter of AIDS cases are contracted through intravenous drug use. Drug users share infected needles because hypodermic needles are illegal and difficult to obtain. Making them legal would virtually end this huge portion of the AIDS epidemic.

9. *Prison space*. Drug users in prison take up room that could be used for violent criminals, who pose a much greater threat to society. Sending a drug offender to prison for one year is equivalent to freeing a violent criminal to commit
   - 40 robberies
   - 7 assaults
   - 110 burglaries
   - 25 auto thefts[16]

10. *Cost*. The nation has spent over $70 billion in two decades on the antidrug war. Yet the drug problem remains as deadly and as costly as ever. Alcohol and tobacco—which are legal—kill or harm more people than do heroin or cocaine.

CRACKING DOWN: THE BENEFITS OF LAW AND ORDER

THE IDEA

Tough, direct, and real, the "law and order" approach takes an offensive posture. It starts with the recognition that only limited resources are available to combat drug use. Therefore, the nation must set its priorities. And clearly, the priority must be using law enforcement.

The approach has two objectives:

- *Cut supply.* To curtail the supply of drugs by cutting foreign drug production, preventing importing of drugs, and imprisoning drug dealers.
- *Cut demand.* To reduce the demand for drugs by making known the penalties for buying and using drugs.

THE DETAILS

The law-and-order approach is a three-part crackdown strategy against drugs:

- *Many fronts.* Maintain a strong policy to put political, economic, and military pressure on nations that produce illegal drugs.
- *Tough on dealers.* Step up efforts to apprehend and prosecute drug dealers to the fullest extent of the law.

- *Deterrence*. Work to deter drug use by ensuring that potential drug users know they stand a good chance of being caught if they purchase, possess, or use drugs—and that they will be punished.

THE FRAMEWORK

The law-and-order approach clearly requires a choice: it advocates making law enforcement the priority—even over prevention and treatment. The Reagan administration, for instance, doubled the nation's antidrug budget—75 percent of which went to law enforcement. The Bush administration tripled the budget, but allocated 70 percent of the funds to law enforcement.

THE ARGUMENT

The case for law and order can be made on two grounds:

- The case *for* enforcing the law
- The case *against* legalizing drugs

The Case for Enforcing the Law

1. *Enforcing laws deters drug use.* In the 1980s, for instance, as the government stepped up law-enforcement efforts, drug use fell sharply. The war on drugs

   - deterred people from trying drugs
   - reduced the availability of drugs
   - deterred use among the young
   - cut casual use

   In one study, seven in ten children cited this as the major reason they don't use drugs: fear of getting in trouble with the law.[17]

2. *Law enforcement keeps drug prices high.* Thanks to the law, drugs cost a lot. And high prices dissuade many people from trying drugs. If antidrug laws were loosened or eliminated, prices would plummet and use would skyrocket. A single dose of crack would retail for as little as forty cents.[18]

3. *Strict enforcement would prevent stronger drugs.* Any reduction in law-enforcement efforts would give drug abusers freer reign; more

abusers would seek ever stronger, more destructive highs.

4. *Destructive behavior.* Drug use leads to irresponsible behavior and violent crime. It must be strictly curtailed.

5. *Laws force rehabilitation.* Tough, no-nonsense law enforcement will force drug abusers to stick with tough drug-treatment programs. Drug laws insist that users commit to rehabilitation to qualify for release or parole—and this saves thousands of lives each year.[19]

6. *Laws prevent use.* Cocaine, heroin, and marijuana were legally available in the United States in the late nineteenth and early twentieth centuries. At that time, America (with half of today's population) produced as many addicts as there are today. But after criminalization, the number dropped to fifty thousand by 1940.[20]

    Finally, the prohibition of alcohol in the 1920s clearly worked to curb the use of alcohol; the rate of its use among Americans has tripled since its repeal.

The Case Against Making Drugs Legal

1. *Legalizing drugs wouldn't cut crime.* Legalizing drugs would do no good. Criminals would simply switch from committing crimes to support their illegal habits to committing crimes to support their *legal* habits. And drug traffickers wouldn't simply go straight— they'd move to new areas of criminal activity. Finally, the increased availability of drugs that impair judgment and self-control would likely spur a wave of violent crime.

2. *Making drugs legal wouldn't eliminate the harmful consequences of drug use.* More readily available drugs would most likely mean more deadly side effects:

    • More drug-driven child abuse
    • More infants born to drug-dependent mothers
    • More violent crime unrelated to obtaining drugs[21]

3. *Looser drug laws in other countries have failed.* Nearly every country that has liberalized its drug policies has suffered for the decision:

    • *Spain.* During the Franco regime, Spain had some of the world's strictest drug laws. They were loosened when the Socialists came to power, leading to a major drug problem. Now, Spain has begun to reestablish tougher drug laws.

- *Italy.* Due to record-high possession, use, and overdose rates, Italy rescinded its "soft" antiheroin laws.
- *Great Britain.* British doctors were at one time allowed to prescribe heroin to patients. But heroin showed up in huge supply on the black market. And after increased drug problems the nation cracked down with stricter, tougher drug policies.[22]

4.   *The devastating effect of crack is a strike against legalization.* Crack sells for about three dollars per dose. It's easy to obtain. Nevertheless, users turn to lives of violent crime to support their habits.

PREVENTION, EDUCATION, AND TREATMENT _____

THE IDEA
The real drug problem may be the simple demand for drugs. How can America cut the demand? By educating Americans about the dangers of narcotics—and by providing effective treatment to those who need to quit abusing drugs.

Again, it's a choice: Given the limited resources available, what should the priority be? Maybe it's not arresting criminals or facing up to foreign governments. Maybe it's teaching Americans about what's best for their bodies.

THE DETAILS
In six basic steps, America's drug problem could be checked. This comprehensive plan educates, prevents, and rehabilitates—it addresses all aspects of American life. The six-step plan seeks to:

- *Educate.* Provide comprehensive antidrug education to children from kindergarten through the eighth grade.
- *Target.* Offer special, intensive drug education, prevention, and treatment programs to high-risk children.
- *Publicize.* Create and support intense national media campaigns to publicize the negative effects of drug use.
- *Treat.* Make long-term drug-rehabilitation programs readily available to the public.

- *Divert.* Give small-scale offenders a chance to rehabilitate through counseling instead of prison.
- *Help.* Provide intensive drug rehabilitation and treatment options for all prison inmates with drug problems.

THE FRAMEWORK

This view is the middle road. It views "law and order" as one extreme, and legalization as the other. In contrast, this strategy advocates:

- *Better education.* Providing specific programs to educate children and equip them to resist drug use.
- *Better environments.* Creating drug-free schools, workplaces, homes, and public places.

THE ARGUMENT

The case for stressing education, prevention, and treatment can be made on two grounds:

- The War on Drugs has failed.
- Education, prevention, and treatment can succeed.

The War on Drugs Has Failed

1. *Enforcement hasn't reduced supply.* Cocaine remains widely available at ever lower prices.[23] And in 1991, after years of tough enforcement, the flow of drugs into the United States had not declined.[24]

2. *Drug enforcement hasn't raised prices.* What was the price of a kilogram of cocaine in Miami?

   - In 1981: $60,000
   - In 1987: $12,000

3. *The War on Drugs has led to stronger drugs.* The massive law-and-order effort of the eighties only led to an increase in the use of hard-core drugs—the very targets of the campaign. How many Americans used cocaine at least once a week?[25]

   - In 1990: 662,000
   - In 1991: 855,000

Education, Prevention, and Treatment Can Succeed

1. *Laws don't stop drug use—people do.* Drug use will decrease when education increases. People will then naturally choose to avoid drugs. The strongest enemy of drug abuse isn't the law, it's societal intolerance of drug use.

2. *Prison doesn't rehabilitate—drug clinics do.* There is ample evidence that drug-rehabilitation works to steer criminals away from lives of crime. The war on drugs merely serves to put more drug addicts in prison.

3. *Drug treatment works.* Highly structured, residential programs that last a year or longer are the most effective way to treat addiction. These programs have this premise: To overcome addiction, addicts must alter their self-images and worldviews with the help of peer pressure, counseling, and therapy.

   - A survey of one residential drug-rehabilitation program found that 80 percent of those who stay in treatment for at least one year remain drug-free.
   - Nationally, one-third of addicts who undergo three months of treatment remain drug-free a year later. For those who stay in treatment for one year, the rate is two-thirds.
   - Studies show that 85 percent of heroin addicts who remain on methadone treatment stay off heroin permanently.[26]

4. *Treatment for incarcerated drug abusers works.* There is strong evidence that structured, long-term drug programs—followed by community-service programs—can reduce rearrest rates by as much as one-half.[27]

   Despite that figure, few drug abusers who are in prison get treatment.

   - Only one in five incarcerated drug abusers gets treatment at all.
   - Of the 41,000 federal prison inmates with drug problems, only 364 are receiving intensive treatment.[28]

   Two programs have shown promise—the Stay'n Out program and the Cornerstone program.

Founded in 1977, Stay 'n Out has treated more than 1,500 inmates of New York State prisons. Participants live apart from the general prison population, and take part in intensive counseling and group seminars to encourage self-awareness and discipline. *Rearrest rates for participants was one-third lower than for inmates who didn't participate.*[29]

Cornerstone, a therapeutic community for thirty-two prison inmates at the Oregon State Hospital, is modeled on Stay'n Out. *Over a three-year study period, almost half the Cornerstone group had not been convicted of another crime—compared to 25 percent of the other prisoners.*[30]

5. *Programs sending those arrested for drug crimes to treatment— rather than jail—work.* In Miami, the "drug court" program allows drug abusers arrested for first-time felony drug possession to opt for an intensive one-year drug treatment instead of jail. Those who fail to finish the program must return to court for a prison sentence. The results:[31]

    - *Completion.* Two-thirds of the defendants who appear in the court successfully complete treatment.
    - *Success.* Among those who complete treatment, the arrest rate after one year is 3 percent—compared to 30 percent for similar offenders who haven't been through the program.
    - *Savings.* It costs $700 for each participant in the program— compared to $30,000 for a year in the Dade County Jail.

6. *Many successful prevention and education programs for youth exist.* With children, the goal is deterring use as long as possible. The longer the delay, the less likely a child will end up abusing drugs. The best programs are those that help children to understand peer pressure—and teach them how to resist.[32]

    Hundreds of drug-prevention programs have sprung up in recent years—so many that it's difficult to evaluate all of them. But many have been proven successes.

    - *Drug Abuse Resistance Education (DARE).* Uniformed police teach drug prevention in the schools. This is the most commonly utilized prevention program for children, reaching more than five million fifth and sixth graders.

- *Head Start.* Studies show that children who participate in pre-school Head Start perform better, stay in school longer, and are less likely to turn to drugs. (Still, Congress has allotted less than half the $7.5 billion annually needed to reach every eligible child.)
- *Life Skills Training (LAST).* Utilized in New York and New Jersey junior high schools for over a decade, LAST teaches children how to make decisions, solve problems, and avoid the social pressures to experiment with drugs. Four-year follow-up studies report that tobacco and marijuana use are one-half to three-quarters lower among LAST students than among those who have not participated.
- *Students' Awareness and Resistance (STAR).* Taught in more than five hundred schools, STAR combines classroom teaching with a larger strategy involving the family, the media, and the community. It teaches "resistance skills" to junior high students, and cuts tobacco, marijuana, and alcohol use by 20 to 40 percent, compared to rates for children who don't participate.

Hundreds of other programs—many of them highly successful—exist. Unfortunately, many school administrators, already overburdened, have failed to incorporate the programs into their curricula.

7. *Antidrug media campaigns have proven successful.* Through the end of 1991, 8,600 Anti-Drug Partnership TV spots had aired—about half during prime time. The ads encourage hostility toward marijuana, cocaine, and crack. They make drug use look unattractive. Studies have shown that these advertisements have substantially altered public attitudes about drugs—especially among teenagers.[33]

DRUG TESTING

On its own, drug testing won't do much. But it serves to augment all of the primary antidrug strategies one supports.

It's indisputable: drug testing is effective. It can save employers billions of dollars in lost productivity.

But is it worth the sacrifice it requires? Many view testing as invasive, intrusive—in short, an assault on civil liberties. The question: Is the invasion of privacy and its chilling effect worth the financial gain?

The tests. What can drug tests determine?[34]

- Marijuana use can be detected for several weeks.
- Cocaine and amphetamines can be traced for more than forty-eight hours.
- Heroin can be identified two to four days after use.

Who gets tested? As the drug scourge has grown, so has the use of drug tests to weed out drug users.

- More than two million federal employees are subject to testing.
- The Department of Defense requires that all defense contractors establish drug programs, including testing.
- Two-thirds of the largest U.S. companies (with more than five thousand employees) conduct testing.

Testing works. The use of drug tests appears to be effective in driving drugs out of the workplace.

- After starting testing, the armed services sharply cut drug use—from 27 percent to 5 percent.
- Positive preemployment drug tests at Southern California Edison, a major power utility, dropped from 26 percent in 1985 to fewer than 1 percent in 1990.

Random testing. Many companies have instituted universal random testing—a way of randomly testing everyone in the organization. The strategy has proven effective. At Texas Instruments, which uses universal random testing, fewer than 1 percent of employees test positive. (Those who test positive are referred to treatment programs and retested later.)

Testing the poor. Some advocates of drug testing have suggested requiring drug tests of all those receiving public assistance. They argue that since the poor are much more likely to become hard-core drug abusers, such a practice would benefit them and attack the drug problem at its core.

THE PEOPLE'S CHOICE

THE PROBLEM

The explosion of the use and abuse of drugs has had shattering effects on American society. Drugs lead to urban blight, tear apart families, afflict schools, aid the spread of AIDS, and ruin countless lives. The government spent $11.9 billion last year on federal anti-drug programs. Combined with state and local costs, the total was over $28 billion. According to the National Institute on Drug Abuse, drug abuse in the workplace alone costs employers $100 billion annually.

SOLUTION I: LAW AND ORDER

THE IDEA

The only way we can overcome the scourge of drugs is to commit ourselves to an all-out war on illegal drug production, distribution, sales, and use.

THE DETAILS

- *Enforcement.* Give priority to the law-and-order aspect of the War on Drugs—making prevention and treatment secondary.
- *Interdiction.* Maintain a strong interdiction policy that puts political, economic, and military pressure on nations producing illegal drugs.
- *Dealers.* Strengthen efforts to apprehend and prosecute drug dealers.
- *Deterrence.* Maintain a credible deterrent, so potential drug users know they will be caught and punished.

SOLUTION II: DRUG LEGALIZATION

THE IDEA

The drug problem—with its related crime, violence, disease, and death—is largely the result of the very laws that seek to eradicate drug use.

THE DETAILS

Simply making drugs legal would have many benefits:

- *Black market.* Legalization would eliminate the black market for drugs overnight.
- *Crime.* Legalization would eliminate most of the crime caused by addicts trying to get drug money.
- *Health.* Legalization would eliminate many sanitary and medical problems associated with drugs. (It's estimated that 80 percent of all drug overdoses stem from problems with illegal drugs, not the effects of the drugs themselves.)
- *Regulation.* Drugs would be placed in the same category as alcohol and tobacco—strongly regulated by the government.

SOLUTION III: EDUCATION, PREVENTION, AND TREATMENT

THE IDEA

Divert most antidrug money and effort toward prevention and treatment programs; law-and-order measures alone can't eradicate the drug problem.

THE DETAILS

- *Education.* Provide timely and effective antidrug education from kindergarten through high school.
- *High-risk kids.* Target high-risk children with especially intensive programs.
- *Media.* Create and support intense national media campaigns to educate the public about drugs.
- *Rehabilitation.* Provide public long-term drug-rehabilitation programs to all Americans with drug problems who seek help.
- *Offenders.* Create rehabilitation and counseling programs—in lieu of jail time—for individuals arrested for possession or use of small amounts of drugs.
- *Prisons.* Provide intensive drug-rehabilitation options for all prison inmates with drug-abuse problems.

ADDENDUM PROPOSITION: DRUG TESTING_____

1. *Employment Testing.* Do you support the expansion of drug testing in the workplace to require drug tests for all job applicants and random testing for all employees?

    Favor [   ]   Oppose [   ]

2. *Testing for Public Aid.* Do you support preregistration testing for recipients of public assistance, as well as ongoing random testing for such recipients?

    Favor [   ]   Oppose [   ]

3. *Testing Students.* Do you support random drug tests for high school students (with results shared with parents and school counselors) so that children and teenagers beginning to experiment with illegal drugs can be identified and routed toward the appropriate counseling and treatment programs?

    Favor [   ]   Oppose [   ]

☆

If the government had as much resolve as the people on the issue of drugs, the problem would be solved. Americans demand: Act now and act with determination.

On no issue were the choices as clear and distinctive as on the question of what to do about the nation's drug problem.

There is nearly universal agreement that something must be done—that the drug scourge is threatening our safety, our schools, our neighborhoods—and our kids' future.

Does that sense of urgency mean we need a radical departure from the strategy that has developed over the past decade?

Americans say: No.

A MATTER OF GOOD AND EVIL

The operative point was this: Most Americans simply see taking drugs as immoral activity. If you're trying to get rid of an immoral activity, what do you do?

Whatever the arguments, Americans can't bring themselves to legalize drugs. They see that as condoning immorality.

And they can't agree to treat drugs as a simple health problem—so the prevention option doesn't hold much attraction.

Americans are of this mind on the drug issue.

- Law and order: 50 percent
- Education, prevention, and treatment: 36 percent
- Legalization: 13 percent

187

DEAD WRONG

The question is: Isn't that just lending support to a failed policy? Americans answer: The problem isn't in the idea behind the policy, it's in how it's been executed. The message is that our society must stand up to the immorality of drugs. We must not give in and admit defeat. And we ought to work for prevention and treatment. But our highest priority must be simply to stand up to behavior that's wrong and—in unquestioning terms—say it's wrong.

PARTY LINES

Americans aren't wholly united in their resolve to make law and order the highest priority in facing up to the drug problem. In fact, the issue divides along party lines. Clearly, party politics has a lot to do with the nation's lack of resolve on the issue.

- *Law and order:*
  - 65 percent of Republicans
  - 35 percent of Democrats
- *Education, prevention, and treatment:*
  - 51 percent of Democrats
  - 23 percent of Republicans

TESTING AND RIGHTS

In fact, Americans view drugs as so immoral—as such a danger to society—that they are willing to forgo other rights to prevent their use. Drugs have had such a catastrophic impact on America that they are willing to have their privacy invaded—and to invade the privacy of others—to ferret out the menace.

For public assistance. How many Americans say anyone receiving public assistance should have to undergo drug screening? Eighty-one percent.

In schools. How many Americans support random drug testing for high school students—to find kids experimenting with drugs and route them to treatment programs? Eighty percent.

At work. How many Americans support expanding workplace drug testing to include preemployment tests and random testing of all employees? Seventy-eight percent.

SACRIFICING FOR THE CAUSE

Clearly, Americans take the drug problem seriously. The people's reactions reflect fear and concern, as well as a collective sense that not enough has been done. But what's most striking is that Americans take the problem so seriously that they're willing to give up rights and compromise their privacy if it will make a difference in creating a drug-free society.

★

III

ISSUES OF SACRIFICE AND COMMITMENT

A	THE DEFICIT
B	AIDS
C	POVERTY
D	HOMELESSNESS
E	THE ENVIRONMENT
F	THE PEOPLE SPEAK

★

On some things, we agree.

But what are we willing to do?

America remains a nation of compassion. Of dedication. Of hope. And despite our divisions, some issues bring us together. Some goals lend unity of purpose.

The problem is, we can't do everything; we have limited resources. There's only so much to go around. The question is: What should the priorities be?

Lip service won't resolve crises. This section is about making choices. It's about sacrifice and commitment. We didn't just acknowledge the problems. We asked the tough questions—point blank. We've demanded that Americans tell us: What will you *do?* What will you *contribute?*

- *Sacrifice.* What are we willing to give up in the name of fixing a societal ailment?
- *Commitment.* How much are we willing to contribute— in time, effort, and money—to solve the nation's problems?

It's one thing to be compassionate, to feel the pain of our fellow citizens. But it's simply naive to think we can cure every ill. We've got to make decisions.

THE ISSUES

No one disagrees that these crises pose serious, visible, and universal challenges to the nation. They're the most insidious problems, and those most difficult to combat. These are the problems that simply won't go away until we decide how much effort we're willing to put out.

The Deficit. It's simple: we're spending more than we're taking in. Everyone agrees we must control the deficit before it wreaks destruction on our economy. We're quick to place blame, but we asked, in real terms: Are Americans willing to make real sacrifices to curb the problem?

193

AIDS. No longer isolated scourges, AIDS and HIV now afflict hundreds of thousands of our citizens. Americans have acknowledged the tragedy. We went beyond the grief and tears. We asked: What are you willing to do to stop the plague?

Poverty. Three decades ago, America launched a "War on Poverty," recognizing the indigent among us and making them an urgent priority. As much as ever, the poor are with us. Yet the nation's leaders seem more focused on the ailing middle class. We asked: Is there commitment behind our compassion? In the wealthiest nation on earth, do we still care about the needy? And how do we show it?

Homelessness. It's poverty with a face—the people we see on our street corners, in alleyways, on stoops. Perhaps our resolve to end this scourge emerges less from compassion than from a desire to get it out of sight. Americans want to end homelessness—but how much? What would they give up to guarantee everyone a home?

The Environment. Once a concern of only an enlightened few, the environment—the earth—has become a topic of mainstream concern and consensus. Americans agree: We've got to preserve the earth, to clean up the air and water, to take care of our natural resources. There's agreement—up to a point. We asked: How far? Is the earth worth paying for? Is nature worth giving up jobs?

SACRIFICE AND COMMITMENT

We'll take a look at each of these issues, then consider what Americans are willing to do to combat them—how much we'd pay in taxes, what sort of personal effort we'd make. We'll pose the question: What are you willing to sacrifice?

First we'll lay out all five issues, then assess how Americans would approach the entire group.

THE DEFICIT

If they could videotape it and put it on the evening news—if the devastation it brings could be put in a picture and beamed into every American's living room, then maybe we'd feel compelled to do something about it.

The deficit is invisible. But it's destroying America.

We don't see its disastrous impact on the streets. We can't feel it or touch it. It's just a bunch of numbers—billions and trillions—numbers we can't begin to grasp.

It was the hot issue of the 1992 presidential campaign. But what happened? Not much. Even the most optimistic versions of President Clinton's budget plans trim only a tiny percentage from the deficit.

It's robbing us of our nation's wealth. And—like some mutant sci-fi movie blob—it's virtually unstoppable.

Watch it grow. Every year, the United States spends far more than it takes in. The result: staggering annual deficits. How high?

- What was the total annual deficit?
  - In 1980: $74 billion
  - In 1992: $292 billion
  - In 1993: $327 billion
- And what will it be?
  - In 1998: $500 billion (projected).
  - In 2000: $1 trillion (projected).[1]
- What was the total accumulated federal debt?
  - In 1980: $908 billion
  - In 1992: $4 trillion
  - In 1993: $4.4 trillion

Staggering figures. In 1990, the total accumulated debt was more than 59 percent of the gross national product.

HOW DID IT HAPPEN?

Deficit spending has long been a fact of life, but through the 1970s, the government was able to maintain relatively modest debts. But from 1980 to 1990, both the annual deficit and the total national debt more than doubled.

Two damaging factors have collaborated to thrust the nation into the red:

- Expanding mandatory federal spending programs
- The economic slowdown

No way out. The government has made it virtually impossible to control its own spending. Why? Because more and more, the federal government has shifted its budget from *discretionary* programs to *mandatory* programs. The difference: discretionary programs must be approved every year; mandatory programs kick in automatically. What proportion of federal spending was mandatory?

- In 1965: 34 percent
- Now: 64 percent

What are the mandatory programs? The biggest aren't welfare programs for the poor. For the most part, they're entitlement programs for the *middle class* and the *elderly*. The largest: Social Security and health-care programs (including Medicare and Medicaid). How much of federal spending goes to health care?

- In 1965: less than 1 percent
- In 1993: 20 percent
- In 1998: 30 percent (projected)

The vicious circle. The most insidious mandatory expense of all? Interest payments on the national debt. How much of federal spending goes to pay interest on the national debt?

- In 1993: 13.4 percent
- In 1998: 16.2 percent (projected)[2]

Stunted growth. If you kept earning less and less money, but spending more and more every year, it would happen to you: you'd run up a huge bill.

And so has America.

It's a numbers game: as long as the economy was growing faster than the deficit, the government could keep the debt in check. The problem: the deficit keeps growing, and federal income (from taxes) keeps shrinking.

- Between 1950 and 1990, how much did the gross national product grow?
  - 268 percent
- In the same period, how much did federal spending grow?
  - 328 percent

With those figures, the equation is clear; we're simply not keeping up. We're taking in less and less money—and spending more and more.

BATTLING THE DEFICIT MONSTER

Deficit spending isn't some farfetched, complex scheme. It's a simple equation: The government keeps spending more than it earns. The potential solutions are as straightforward as the problem:

- Raise taxes
- Cut spending
- A combination: raise taxes and cut spending

It's that basic. So what's kept the nation from curbing the deficit? We're paralyzed; we can't agree on what to do. Liberals want to raise taxes. Conservatives want to cut spending. And the people don't want to sacrifice on either end.

OPTION NO. 1: RAISE TAXES

The pros: More money in the national coffers.

The cons:

- Americans don't like paying taxes and don't reelect leaders who raise their taxes.
- Taking money out of the economy can stifle economic growth.

OPTION NO. 2: CUT SPENDING

The pros: More money in the national coffers.
   The cons: There's no fat to cut.
   What does the government spend its money on?

- 27 percent: national defense
- 40 percent: social insurance programs (e.g., Social Security)
- 14 percent: interest on the debt
- 19 percent: everything else

So where can the government cut spending?

- *Defense?* The consensus is, the nation can't cut defense spending much more and remain the leader of the free world.
- *Social insurance?* Cutting programs that benefit the middle class is political suicide for leaders.
- *Debt payments?* Defaulting on debt payments would damage the nation's credit rating—and the United States couldn't borrow any more money.
- *Other programs?* There's virtually no way to cut spending without angering a significant segment of Americans—maybe enough to drive leaders out of office.

The Democrats talk about tax hikes—but not large enough increases to make a difference. The Republicans consider draconian spending cuts, but won't take the political risk of cutting social insurance programs.

OPTION NO. 3: THE FLEXIBLE FREEZE

A final, more realistic approach acknowledges that there's a slim chance that either tax hikes or program hikes will add up enough to overcome the deficit. The "flexible freeze" approach—championed by Michael Boskin, who chaired President Bush's Council of Economic Advisers—

is a simple formula: Reduce the rate of *spending growth* to below the rate of *economic growth,* and the deficit will slowly fade away.

"LET'S GET UNDER THE HOOD"

Are the American people simply too weak, or too afraid, to make the sacrifices necessary to balance the books? Ross Perot, in his celebrated presidential candidacy, made one convincing statement: It's not the people who are afraid; it's the *politicians.*

For all his failings, Perot has shown admirable faith in the people's strength, resilience, and willingness to make sacrifices for the good of the nation. Perot's plan comes down to twelve crucial points:

1. *Cut discretionary spending* by enacting across-the-board cuts.
2. *Enact the line-item veto,* allowing the president to trim excesses from legislation without killing the entire bill.
3. *Enact a deficit-reduction law,* requiring Congress to stay within set limits.
4. *Eliminate special favors* to interest groups, which cost Americans about $50 billion annually.
5. *Cut the defense budget* to meet its mission in the wake of the Cold War's end.
6. *Stop subsidizing the rich* by raising their tax rates and eliminating various tax exemptions.
7. *Control entitlement costs* by having users of Medicare and other programs pay a higher proportion of program costs, taxing Social Security benefits, and reining in federal pension increases.
8. *Raise tobacco and gas taxes.*
9. *Make tax collection more effective* by ridding the IRS of costly inefficiencies.
10. *Force our allies to share the burden of defense,* recognizing that we can't pay to protect other nations anymore.
11. *Tame health-care costs* with a national board to oversee health-care reform.
12. *Control the cost of governing* by eliminating the air fleets used exclusively by the government, cutting congressional staffs and perks, and reforming campaign spending laws.

NO PAIN, NO GAIN

Though President Clinton pays lip service to the problem, his actions have been ineffectual. Tackling the deficit will require such a radical restructuring of the way government taxes and spends that middle-of-the-road options simply won't do. To succeed, any approach will have to inflict a certain amount of pain. President Clinton's economic plans have given serious consideration to reducing deficit spending—but not to doing anything about the huge deficit that has accumulated over the last two decades.

AIDS

Out of nowhere came an epidemic.

Fifteen years ago, AIDS was unheard of. It has spread through the population with frightening speed and with shattering impact.

"It can't happen to me." That is the thinking that keeps America from focusing its attention on this cruel and merciless killer. Predictably, those who feel most immune from AIDS, most protected from its impact, are those least likely to make it a priority.

The truth is that no one is immune. Sadly, it may take that realization to bring enough attention to make a difference.

The disease is hitting home in tragic proportions. Americans once thought AIDS was one of those things that happened only to other people. No more. The revelation that basketball star Magic Johnson has HIV, the virus responsible for AIDS, heightened public awareness. But on a smaller scale, the disease was already felt. By 1991, 13 percent of Americans had known someone with AIDS.[1]

AIDS is now the leading cause of death for American men between ages fifteen and forty-four.[2]

The most tragic and devastating statistic about AIDS is the certainty of its impact: It will kill 100 percent of those it afflicts.

HOW WIDESPREAD?

How many Americans are affected by AIDS?[3]

- *HIV.* Between 1 million and 1.5 million Americans carry the HIV virus, which causes AIDS.
- *AIDS.* As of February 1993, 253,448 Americans suffered from full-blown AIDS.

201

- *Deaths.* AIDS has killed more than 350,000 people in the United States.

The future of AIDS looks more frightening than the past.[4]

- By 1994, 511,000 will have been diagnosed with AIDS.
- In 1993 and 1994, between 92,000 and 141,000 will die from AIDS.

WHO GETS AIDS?

In the earliest phases of the epidemic, AIDS tended to strike gay men and people who use intravenous drugs. As long as it stayed on the fringe, it was easy for those in the political mainstream to virtually ignore it. Those groups still account for the majority of victims, but heterosexuals increasingly feel the plague's effects.

Who gets AIDS?[5]

- 58 percent: Gay/bisexual men (non–IV users)
- 25 percent: Heterosexuals (IV users)
- 9 percent: Heterosexuals (contracted through sex)
- 6 percent: Gay/bisexual men (IV users)
- 1.5 percent: Infants (through prenatal transmission)

Minorities. Members of minority groups are affected with AIDS in disproportionate numbers:[6]

- *African-Americans* make up 12 percent of the population, but 28 percent of AIDS cases.
- *Hispanics* are 8 percent of the population, but 16 percent of AIDS cases.

Women. Is AIDS a disease that affects only men? No. The younger the woman, the more likely she is to be affected with AIDS.

- How many people with AIDS are female (overall)?[7] One in nine.
- Of AIDS sufferers in their twenties, how many are female? One in four.

In fact, AIDS is far from unheard of among women: it's the fifth leading cause of death among women between fifteen and forty-four.[8]

Children. More and more, the people with the disease are children. Nationwide, nearly 3,600 people under thirteen suffer from AIDS.

- How did they get it?
  - 85 percent prenatally
  - 13 percent through blood transfusions
- Who are they?
  - 52 percent are black
  - 25 percent are Hispanic
  - 22 percent are white

A DEAD END

Once you acquire HIV, it's virtually guaranteed that AIDS will kill you.

Treatment. Aren't new drugs helping? Yes, but not curing. AZT, for instance, helps people with AIDS to live longer and healthier lives.

- Life expectancy for person contracting AIDS: 140 days
- Expectancy if treated with AZT: 770 days

Prevention. The best way for Americans to keep the epidemic in check is to be aware of the disease. Yet only 29 percent of Americans have been tested for the HIV virus. Why? Even with the disease surrounding us, we still don't feel vulnerable. Of those who haven't been tested, 84 percent said they don't consider themselves to be at risk.[9]

PAYING THE BILL

The greatest cost of AIDS is the ever-growing loss of life—mostly people struck down in the prime of their lives. But as the disease spreads, it is also becoming a larger and larger financial burden.

Currently, it costs about $60,000 per patient to treat AIDS.[10] What's the medical bill for treating all Americans with HIV?[11]

- In 1993: $11.8 billion
- In 1994: $13.5 billion
- In 1995: $15.2 billion

Those costs add up to frightening figures. By the year 2000, AIDS will absorb as much as $107 billion from the U.S. economy.[12]

FEDERAL HELP

Congress first allotted federal money to battle AIDS in 1982. As the disease has spread, the amount of federal spending to fight AIDS has grown:

- In 1982: $5.6 million
- In 1993: $2 billion

Although these figures reveal a striking increase in money set aside to combat the disease, the numbers are deceiving. Since 1988, the *growth* in government spending on AIDS has slowed considerably.

- Annual increase in U.S. AIDS funding:
    - In 1987: 115 percent
    - In 1991: 19 percent
    - In 1993: 6 percent

Why has the flow of money slowed down—when the disease hasn't? In fact, AIDS continues to spread exponentially. But despite the media's continuing attention to the issue, and the high-profile cases of Magic Johnson, Arthur Ashe, and others, the disease simply hasn't been able to compete with other problems and programs for federal dollars.

POVERTY

In the wealthiest nation on earth, do we feel an obligation to take care of the indigent? Do we make it a priority to take care of the underprivileged?

The fact is, the public can make a difference. When we decide to take care of our own, we get it done.

In the 1960s, we declared war on poverty. The results show that the initiative of leaders can indeed change things. Did we win? We still have poor among us, but the fight made a difference. What percentage of Americans lived in poverty?[1]

- In 1959: 22.5 percent
- In 1973: 11.1 percent

THE GOOD NEWS

Clearly, the national effort worked to change society. In fact, almost any way you look at it, poverty has been slashed since the 1950s.

- Among female-headed familes:
  - In 1959: 42.5 percent
  - In 1990: 33.4 percent
- Black children:
  - In 1959: 66 percent
  - In 1990: 44.7 percent
- White children:
  - In 1959: 20.6 percent
  - In 1990: 15.6 percent[2]

The elderly: a great leap. Historically, the elderly have been the segment of the population hardest hit by poverty. But new programs—such as cost-of-living adjustments to Social Security, the Supplemental Security Income program, and private pensions—have slashed the poverty rate among older Americans from 35.2 percent in 1959 to 12.2 percent in 1990.[3]

THE BAD NEWS

But those figures show a distorted picture of progress. The War on Poverty steadily worked away at bringing aid to the indigent until the 1980s, when poverty rose once again.

- Family poverty:
    - 1959: 18.5 percent
    - 1974: 8.8 percent
    - 1983: 12.3 percent[4]

The family poverty rate fell again—in 1990 it stood at 10.7 percent—but it has never returned to the low point of the mid-1970s. The nation simply hasn't made it a priority.

WHO ARE THE POOR?

Poverty affects all types, but there's a pattern: those with the least power are the most likely to be poor.

Women. Women consistently earn less money than men—typically, about 60 percent of their male counterparts. Yet they often bear the burden of raising children in broken families. The result is striking: 65 percent of the adult poor are women.[5]

Families headed by women. With the increasing corrosion of family structures, more and more families are headed by women—especially among minority groups. (Of black families with dependent children, 53 percent are headed by women.) Because of the burdens placed on such women—and their unequal earning status—these families suffer disproportionately from poverty.

Among families with children under eighteen, how many are in poverty?

- 7.8 percent of those headed by married couples
- 18.8 percent of those headed by single males
- 44.5 percent of those headed by single females

Among black families, how many are in poverty?

- 14.3 percent of those headed by married couples
- 27.3 percent of those headed by single males
- 56 percent of those headed by single females[6]

Children. Youths under thirteen make up the largest segment of the American poor.

- One in five children lives in poverty.
- 40 percent of the poor are children (compared to 24 percent of the nonpoor).[7]

Minorities. Members of minority groups are far more likely than whites to be living below the poverty level. While only about one in ten whites lives in poverty, the figures for minorities are striking:

- Blacks: 31 percent
- Hispanics: 28 percent[8]

The working poor. From 1979 to 1984, most (60 percent) of the new jobs created in the United States paid less than $7,000 annually.[9] Despite the persistent myth that the poor are unproductive elements of society, millions of the poor actually hold jobs.

- 60 percent of able-bodied adults living in poverty work part-time, full-time, or seasonally.[10]
- 71 percent of poor children live in families with one or both parents working.[11]

WHAT ARE WE DOING ABOUT POVERTY?

The numbers are deceiving. We're spending more on welfare programs— but getting less for the money. In the 1980s, per-capita welfare spending fell, and welfare spending failed to keep pace with inflation.[12]

Cash/noncash. Welfare programs can be divided into two varieties—those that pay cash to recipients, and those that don't.

Aid to Families with Dependent Children (AFDC). About eleven million people in four million families benefit from AFDC, which is financed by the federal government (54 percent) and individual states. The program generally aids needy families with absentee parents.

Supplementary Security Income (SSI). The SSI program sends monthly payments to 4.5 million people. The federal government pays about 78 percent of the cost. SSI benefits the needy elderly, blind, and disabled.

Medicaid. Most AFDC and SSI recipients qualify for Medicaid, the medical coverage program, which is the largest noncash welfare program.

Food stamps. About nineteen million Americans receive an average of $600 annually in food stamps, at a cost to the government of about $11.4 billion.

Despite these programs, the poor are only getting poorer. Between 1970 and 1992, average AFDC and food stamp benefits for a mother of two with no income *fell by 25 percent.*[13]

HOMELESSNESS

Does an American have the right to a home?

That is the fundamental question of the issue of homelessness. Until the early 1980s, homelessness seemed limited to a few fringe individuals—the persistent poor, living on skid rows. Today, most Americans living in big cities—76 percent, according to *The New York Times*—see the homeless as part of their everyday routines.

The question remains: Do the homeless choose their plight? Is it a sort of lifestyle choice? Or is society to blame for not taking care of its own?

Before we tackled those questions, we started with the basics.

HOW MANY?

Homelessness has become such a hotly debated political issue that it's easier to get distorted figures than accurate counts of how many Americans are without shelter. The estimates range from 300,000 to 3 million. But several estimates provide a reliable range.

- Peter Rossi, prominent sociologist: 300,000 to 500,000 on any given night[1]
- The Bipartisan Institute: 567,000 to 600,000 total
- Gordon Berliner and William McAllister, experts on homelessness: 500,000 on any given night[2]

A GROWING MENACE

Whatever the actual numbers of homeless, there is a general consensus that they are rising:

- In 1984: 250,000
- In 1988: 600,000[3]

The increasing numbers have been reflected in ever greater demands. In recent years, the demand for emergency shelter has climbed by an average of 30 percent annually.

WHO ARE THE HOMELESS?

The most striking fact about the homeless: they're shockingly poor. What's the monthly income (all sources) for the homeless?

- Single adults: less than $150
- Families: about $350

Beyond that basic poverty, the homeless population falls into three groups:

- *The unfortunate.* About 15 percent are people who are simply down on their luck.
- *The mentally ill.* About one third are people with mental disorders. (Twice as many schizophrenics are in public shelters as in state hospitals.)
- *Abusers.* About half are alcoholics and drug addicts.

WHAT CAUSES HOMELESSNESS?

How has our society come to a point where homelessness is tolerated and accepted as a fact of life? That is the political question. But what about individuals? What explains why any given American might end up on the street?

Are the homeless lazy? Are they victims? Are they ill?

The answer: They are all of these. Obviously, no single factor can explain the fates of thousands of people. Eric Rubenstein, whose organization, the Single Room Operators Association, works to provide affordable housing, suggests an eclectic list of twenty reasons.

1. Questionable values
2. Antisocial behavior
3. Loss or lack of financial resources
4. Mental illness
5. Cutbacks in welfare money
6. Physical abuse at home
7. Lack of alternative housing
8. Poor money management
9. Acquiring a "homeless mentality"
10. Drug abuse
11. Pure laziness
12. Evictions
13. Alcohol abuse
14. Chronic health problems
15. Lack of affordable housing
16. Failed government programs
17. The rescinding of vagrancy laws
18. Restrictive building and zoning codes
19. Unrealistic job expectations
20. Fires and building condemnation

ONE RESPONSE: GET ANGRY

More and more, Americans are reacting to homelessness not by trying to solve the problems, but by getting angry at the homeless. The homeless have become such a presence in our cities that citizens have taken action not to provide aid, but simply to get the homeless out of the way:

- New York has evicted the homeless from Tompkins Square Park.
- Chicago has shut O'Hare Airport to the homeless.
- Santa Barbara has banned sleeping on public streets.
- Atlanta is considering making "aggressive begging" a crime.[4]

ANOTHER RESPONSE: EXPLORE
THE CAUSES

Pushing homeless people out of the way won't solve the problem; it will just make it fester unseen. Philip Kasinitz, a leading urban sociologist, suggests five basic alternatives in the fight to end homelessness:

1. Reinstitutionalize the mentally ill
2. Create more public housing
3. Eliminate rent control
4. Make housing a political right
5. Do nothing

OPTION NO. 1: BACK TO THE INSTITUTIONS _____

THE PROBLEM

Up through the 1950s, people with serious mental disabilities were generally placed in mental institutions. Since the 1960s, however, these people have been moved from institutions and granted greater freedom. Their support, it was believed, could come from community-based mental health services.

But taking them out of institutions failed. Why? Very few communities have offered services and homes for these recently discharged mental patients.

- In Massachusetts, a hospital reported that 27 percent of patients were homeless within six months of release.
- In Ohio, a hospital said that more than 36 percent were homeless within six months.[5]

THE SOLUTION

The most obvious response is to put homeless people with manifest mental illnesses in institutions. This would guarantee them shelter, food, and medical and psychiatric care, prevent them from abusing drugs and alcohol, and protect them from crime and violence.

The drawback: Housing and caring for hundreds of thousands of patients would cost billions in tax dollars, and take money from other programs.

OPTION NO. 2: MORE FEDERAL HOUSING ⸻⸻⸻

THE PROBLEM
During the 1980s, cheap housing—specifically, inexpensive, single-room-occupancy hotels—virtually disappeared.

- How many single-room-occupancy hotel units were there in New York City?[6]
  - In 1970: 127,000
  - In 1983: 14,000
- Nationally, how many unsubsidized units with rent and utilities below $300 disappeared between 1974 and 1985?
  - 2.5 million

THE SOLUTION
The federal government should get involved in providing housing. How?

- *Encourage construction of affordable housing* by providing tax incentives to developers.
- *Build more public housing.*
- *Provide single-room-occupancy housing*—perhaps by giving subsidy vouchers to those who can't afford this most basic form of shelter.

The drawbacks: More federal involvement would cost billions in tax dollars, and take money from other programs.

OPTION NO. 3: ELIMINATE RENT CONTROL ⸻⸻⸻

THE PROBLEM
Perhaps the answer to homelessness isn't more government, but less. Ironically, the cities with the toughest rent-control laws are also those

with the greatest housing shortages. Rent control was intended to help the poor, but for many landlords, it's simply made it unprofitable to own property. So landlords have simply abandoned their buildings.

THE SOLUTION

Return the profit motive by rescinding rent-control policies. Ending rent control would immediately stimulate the growth of the rental housing industry.

But wouldn't it just mean more expensive apartments? Perhaps, at first. But the laws of supply and demand would eventually bring the prices down to reasonable rates.

The benefits: It wouldn't cost taxpayers anything.

The drawbacks: The policy might hurt those it's meant to help; it may cause more homelessness if landlords raise the rents and then evict tenants who can't pay. Rent control may have to be phased out slowly.

OPTION NO. 4: MAKE HOUSING A RIGHT _____

We return to the question we started with: Should housing be a right of every citizen? Perhaps. And perhaps the nation should commit itself to providing a home for every American.

THE SOLUTION

The nation would begin a massive national program to create enough housing to give shelter to every citizen.

The drawbacks: Besides the massive cost to taxpayers, this plan would call for a significant shift in outlook. Most Americans see housing as an individual responsibility; even the most liberal citizens might hesitate to hand over so many of society's resources to those who can't take care of themselves.

OPTION NO. 5: DO NOTHING _____

Why is so little done to help the homeless? Because the majority of Americans simply don't feel the issue threatens them personally.

The homeless aren't a scourge—they're a nuisance. We don't fear them; we just don't like to see them. We don't want to help them obtain housing; we want to help them to disappear.

We're afraid of AIDS, of crime, of drugs. But the homeless are too weak and helpless to do us any harm. In an age of limited resources, we may be compelled to act against the most pressing issues. And homelessness may not get the attention it deserves, simply because it doesn't scare people.

THE ENVIRONMENT

Earth Day. Owls. And recycled garbage.

Are we concerned about the environment?

Certainly. Americans express great interest in issues of pollution, conservation, and toxic waste.

Are we willing to do anything about those issues?

The jury's still out.

SOMETHING NEW IN THE AIR

For a long time, the environment generally was seen as something of a fringe issue, a cause taken up by hippies, animal lovers, and left-wing extremists.

Not anymore.

In the eighties, environmentalism became cool. It also became important—a matter of national concern and focus. Nearly nine out of ten Americans say they consider the environment to be a "very serious" issue.[1]

The media's portrayal of environmentalism as a divisive issue—with industry pitted against liberal conservationists—is extreme. We found a solid consensus in favor of looking after our environment. Eight in ten Americans said that "requirements and standards cannot be too high, and continuing environmental improvements must be made regardless of costs."

A SERIES OF CRISES

Americans don't view the environment as a single issue. Rather, they understand that it's an umbrella—a complex compilation of different problems, each of which presents a serious threat.[2]

- *Air and water:* 90 percent of Americans say government should make it a top priority to clean up the nation's air and water.
- *Recycling:* 87 percent say the government should require citizens to separate household trash for recycling.
- *Toxic chemicals:* 87 percent want stricter controls on the use, transportation, and disposal of toxins.
- *Hazardous waste:* 77 percent call for stricter controls on the disposal of hazardous waste.
- *Acid rain and toxic waste:* 68 percent favor spending tax dollars to combat acid rain and toxic waste dumping.
- *Air pollution:* 56 percent want more stringent controls on air pollution.

TALKING AND DOING

All that concern is heartwarming. The question is: If Americans are so worried about the environment, then why aren't they *doing* anything about it?[3]

- *No activity.* Just one in five Americans has ever participated in any environmental activity.
- *No contributions.* Only 15 percent of Americans have ever given money to an environmental cause.
- *No membership.* Just one in ten citizens belongs to an environmental group.

The gap between words and actions was striking. Nearly 97 percent of Americans express solidarity with environmental causes. But fewer than a quarter were willing to make any real individual sacrifices for the cause.

A SCALE OF COMMITMENT AND ACTION

When it comes to environmental concerns, Americans seem to fall within four groups:[4]

- *Greener-than-greens:* Strong environmental concerns *and* willingness to make significant sacrifices. Total: 23 percent.
- *Greens:* Environmental concerns, but willingness to make only minimal sacrifice. Total: 59 percent.
- *Light greens:* Environmental concerns, but no willingness to make sacrifices. Total: 15 percent.
- *Ungreens:* No environmental concerns *or* willingness to make sacrifices. Total: 3 percent.

THE PEOPLE SPEAK ... ON ISSUES OF SACRIFICE AND COMMITMENT

TALK IS CHEAP

Actions speak louder than words. First, we asked Americans what they *thought*. But we were more interested in what they'd be willing to *do*. For all the talk about how concerned Americans are about the problems vexing the nation, we wanted to know if they were willing to make sacrifices.

We examined the issues of sacrifice and commitment individually— but in solving them, we considered them as a group by asking people: What are you willing to do?

We can combat problems on a small scale—fight homelessness by pitching in at a homeless shelter; help the environment by joining a conservation group. But how would the solutions to these societal problems affect the average American? In short, how do you show your commitment to fixing a problem? In two ways:

- *Paying taxes.* Putting your money where your mouth is.
- *Forgoing benefits.* Sacrificing something else—government programs or individual benefits—for the sake of solving a problem.

A discouraging picture. When we asked Americans how much they were willing to sacrifice to cure the nation's ailments, we found a distressing reality.

Most people already feel the government charges them too much in taxes—and doesn't do enough to help them.

219

PAYING UNCLE SAM

Would people pay more taxes to solve these problems? In virtually every possible way, Americans told us: No!

The message was clear and unambiguous.

- "I already pay too much in taxes." Eighty-two percent agreed.
- "I do not believe that the way to solve America's problems is by raising taxes higher than they already are." Ninety-one percent agreed.

In fact, a large majority of Americans favor *cutting* taxes, not raising them—or even maintaining current levels.

Americans already feel taxed to the hilt. A significant majority—61 percent—said they were unwilling to pay higher taxes themselves to help address the nation's problems.

A minority of Americans—39 percent—said they'd be willing to pay higher taxes. We asked them: What would you pay for?

- To fight the deficit: 9 percent
- To combat AIDS: 5 percent
- To help the poor: 3 percent
- To battle homelessness: 2 percent
- To clean up the environment: 6 percent

Even in the minority who are willing to pay more taxes, three in four said they wouldn't pay them to help solve any of these pressing issues.

A SPIRIT OF SACRIFICE?

If they're not willing to pay more taxes, will Americans tackle these issues by shifting their priorities—by giving up other benefits for the sake of combating these crises?

Don't count on it.

In poll after poll, Americans have said that they favor solving the nation's pressing crises not with new taxes, but by cutting spending.

It's a nice theory.

Americans call for cuts. So we said: Where should we cut? And the answer was: Not where it affects me.

Question: How many Americans are willing to see their own government benefits cut to help solve the nation's pressing problems?

To Help Fight . . .	I'd Sacrifice Money from My . . .					
	Social Security	Medi-care	Veterans Benefits	Medi-caid	Disability Benefits	Unemployment Insurance
Budget Deficit	15%	7%	11%	9%	10%	20%
AIDS	2%	8%	3%	4%	4%	6%
Environment	5%	3%	7%	3%	3%	9%
Homelessness	6%	3%	9%	4%	4%	7%
Poverty	5%	3%	5%	4%	4%	4%

Predictably, few Americans were willing to give up their own benefits—even to fight these urgent issues. So we asked where the cuts might come:

Question: Are you willing to cut benefits for the wealthy to solve the nation's pressing crises?

Problem	Social Security	Medicare
Budget Deficit	63%	41%
AIDS	42%	36%
Environment	49%	33%
Homelessness	49%	35%
Poverty	50%	34%

Question: Are you willing to cut benefits for the poor to solve the nation's pressing crises?

Problem	AFDC Welfare	Food Stamps	Head Start
Budget Deficit	43%	25%	25%
AIDS	26%	15%	9%
Environment	24%	13%	18%
Homelessness	27%	15%	11%
Poverty	32%	13%	12%

Perhaps when the nation felt more prosperity—in the fifties and six-ties—there was more willingness to spread it around. But as the nation suffers economically, the politics of compassion have been replaced by a new set of slogans: Don't look at me. What's in it for me? Don't take it from me.

ANY VOLUNTEERS?

If money's not the answer, maybe something else is. If Americans won't pay more taxes, and if they won't give up benefits, maybe something else can enter the equation: maybe they're willing to give their time and effort.

Or maybe not.

President Bush made the case that the spirit of volunteerism could overcome any problem. If Americans would line up to do AIDS education, to help homeless people find jobs, to staff community recycling programs, maybe it would help fight the problems.

Perhaps, if anyone would volunteer.

Question: What acts of volunteerism or charity have you made in the past year toward combating national problems?

To Help Fight . . .	I've Given Free Time	I've Joined an Organization
Budget Deficit	3%	7%
AIDS	5%	2%
Environment	20%	15%
Homelessness	12%	8%
Poverty	12%	7%

WHOSE JOB IS IT, ANYWAY?

If Americans aren't giving their time and effort to solve the problems, and they aren't willing to give their money, the question arises: Who do we expect to fight these battles? The more we asked, the more we came to understand: Americans rely on the government to solve the pressing issues of the day.

Question: Who has the most responsibility for fixing the nation's crises—the government, business, or Americans?

Problem	Government	Business	Americans
Budget Deficit	94%	0%	5%
Poverty	71%	3%	26%
AIDS	65%	0%	32%
Homelessness	54%	5%	36%
Environment	47%	21%	29%

CONFRONTING HOMELESSNESS

On the homeless issue, we asked Americans to consider five specific solutions. And their reaction fell in line with the more general outlook on this set of problems.

Put them away. Americans rejected an array of options aimed at making it easier for the homeless to find homes. The approach most people favored wasn't a way to help the indigent to make their way back into mainstream society. It was a way to put them further out of sight.

- *Back to the institutions. Seventy percent* of Americans, asked what to do about homelessness, said the answer was to force mentally ill people back into institutions.

CONCLUSION: WHITHER THE SPIRIT OF SACRIFICE?

We won't pay new taxes.

We won't sacrifice any benefits.

We don't take the time and effort to volunteer.

The picture is sobering. Americans recognize the urgent and distressing nature of the problems facing the nation. But what are they willing to do about them?

Next to nothing.

Has the United States become a nation of greedy, uncharitable individuals? Have Americans given up on the idea of pitching in for the common good?

We don't think so.

Should we blame Americans for turning their backs on the national welfare?

We don't. Our research proved again and again that Americans are willing to face their problems—and to do something about them.

We don't blame the people. We blame their leaders.

Leaders don't ask Americans to give—to sacrifice—anymore. They make promises. They tell Americans what they want to hear. They look for the easiest way to get things done—not the hardest.

There was a time when the highest quality of a leader was the ability to rally others to give and sacrifice for the collective good.

Look at the last presidential campaign:

- *Bill Clinton* promised to solve the nation's problems painlessly, by taxing the wealthy.
- *George Bush* wouldn't admit the nation had any serious problems.

In fact, it was Ross Perot who called on Americans to face up to their problems and make individual sacrifices. His honest call to arms had some appeal; his third-party candidacy garnered 20 percent of the vote.

John F. Kennedy made his mark by calling for a spirit of sacrifice. He wasn't a "feel-good" president. He didn't make empty promises or ignore pressing problems. From the beginning, he based his presidency on the notion that Americans had a duty to give to their nation—that the welfare of the nation is dependent not on the government, not on big business, but on the contributions and sacrifices of individual citizens.

When he launched the New Frontier at the 1960 Democratic National Convention, he said his appeal would be: "Not what I intend to offer the American people, but what I intend to ask of them."

Americans didn't take that as a threat. They clung to it as a challenge, a rallying cry. He said in his inaugural speech: "Pay any price, bear any burden, meet any hardship, support any friend, oppose any foe to assure the survival and success of liberty."

Why are Americans unwilling to sacrifice? In large part because their leaders don't ask them to.

We don't have campaigns based on calls to sacrifice anymore. They're based on political expediency, on angry words, on style, on attack ads.

So the spirit of sacrifice comes from the top. We absorb the messages of our leaders. And our leaders have stopped asking us to give. They've stopped asking us to think about others, and conditioned us to ask: What's in it for me?

Here's what we've lost: our faith in a common national destiny. We're alienated from the political process. We're alienated from our neighbors. We need a new spirit of giving, but even more than that, we need leaders with the courage to ask us to give.

★

IV
WEDGE ISSUES

A RACISM

B GUN CONTROL

C ABORTION

D SEXUAL DISCRIMINATION

AND HARASSMENT

★

The media is wrong: America is united.

Watch a talk show. Read an op-ed page. Listen to a radio call-in show. No matter what the issue, it's portrayed in the same light: Left. Right. And nothing in between. Black. White. But no shades of gray. To listen to the media, we're a nation of extremes, a place where conservatives and liberals live side by side, with polarized views of the world and no hope of a truce.

Is that really America? We don't think so.

When we looked behind the hype, when we dug into the issues the media keeps telling us are dividing the country, we found a shocking truth: there's more pulling us together than tearing us apart.

There's an easy explanation: the media likes conflict. It sells newspapers. It grabs ratings. Consider a scenario for a moment. You're flipping through dozens of cable stations in search of something provocative. Do you stop on a program where two amiable commentators are agreeing with each other—nodding approvingly and saying, "You know, I've never thought of it that way!"?

No. That's why it's not on. That's why CNN's *Crossfire* each weeknight shows Michael Kinsley ("from the left") and Patrick Buchanan ("from the right") tearing into each other, boldly disputing absolutely anything that happens in America. And never agreeing.

And that's why the radio dial is loaded with provocative talk-show hosts who start each hour with controversial, polarizing statements, then take call after call from people who either vilify or worship them. Rush Limbaugh never looks for the middle ground. It just wouldn't draw ratings.

In the popular media, everyone screams, and nobody listens.

We didn't think that was America. And when we investigated, it turned out we were right.

We looked into four of the issues—"wedge issues"—the media tells us are tearing America apart:

- Racism
- Gun Control
- Abortion
- Sexual Harassment

What we found is that Americans aren't one-dimensional people, jumping readily into one camp or another:

- We listen to each other.
- We agree more than we disagree.
- We understand the complexity of issues.
- We struggle with vexing, gut-wrenching issues.
- We often come down in the middle, not on the extremes.

You'll never see a TV opinion show with the premise of portraying people grappling with the subtle middle ground on the issues. It just wouldn't sell. Yet that's where most Americans find themselves. And even the true extremists have values in common with those they so bitterly oppose.

In the 1980s, professional political operators coined the term "wedge issues" for matters that are perceived to be dividing the electorate—issues on which one side defines itself as "right" and the other as "wrong." In our view, wedge issues are something quite different—a chance to show that there's hope, that we've made progress, that the nation can explore complex issues in sophisticated ways and try to move forward. Every day, the media finds new sources of conflict; in the same places, we find reason for hope.

RACISM

The question: Unity or division? Hate or tolerance?

The bad news is for the cynical political operators, the hatemongers, and the ideologues on both sides who have made every effort to pit race against race in America, to make us think we're a nation divided along lines of color.

The good news is for America: We're not racists; we're not headed for ethnic war; we're not our neighbors' enemies.

When we went to discover how the races relate in America, the message was clear: We all want unity. We all want brotherhood. We all want peace.

Racial division and fear can still be felt throughout America. The 1988 "Willie Horton ad"—the Bush campaign television advertisement designed to take political advantage of unspoken fears—crystallized the potential for bringing unspoken racial anxiety to the surface. Such efforts give the illusion that Americans want to be divided. What we found is that, in fact, we want to learn to live together.

We just haven't figured out how.

Certainly, Americans have anxieties about racial strife. But we don't hear much about complex feelings or inner conflict. Just hate and violence. We found Americans struggling with racism—to overcome it and to find ways to a more just and equitable society.

We agree on the goal. We're struggling to find a way.

PROGRESS

In the past, racism was institutionalized—an overt, accepted, integral part of American society. The military had separate platoons for blacks and whites; schools were segregated; Jim Crow laws made it difficult for blacks to vote. In the South, blacks were forced to use separate public facilities—water fountains and rest rooms—to ride in separate sections on buses; they were refused service at restaurants and hotels.

No more. The battle for equal rights has been fought. And won. Nearly all Americans now believe in the ideas and laws that call for a society of equality under the law. That much progress has been made.

- *Professional integration.* Eighty-four percent of blacks say they work with a member of another race.[1]
- *Social integration.* Sixty-three percent of blacks regularly socialize with members of other races.[2]

A DIFFICULT FIT

Despite the progress, equality under the law has not given all blacks equal status in society.

As a black insurance broker told Studs Terkel: "Being black in America is like being forced to wear ill-fitting shoes. Some people can bear the uncomfort more than others. Some people can block it from their mind, some can't. When you see some acting docile and some acting militant, they have one thing in common: The shoe is uncomfortable."[3]

TWO TRACKS

As much as the nation yearns for a color-blind society, African-Americans continue to be impoverished in great numbers. The result of civil rights hasn't been equality, but a duality:

- *The upside:* The black middle class has grown greatly, and blacks have taken significant places in mainstream culture.
- *The downside:* Crime, welfare dependency, fragmented families, and drugs have ravaged the black underclass.

As one academic put it, the reality of the black underclass is working to undermine the progress of the black middle class. "The behavior of black males in the underclass is now beginning to look like the black stereotype," wrote Howard University professor Kenneth S. Tollett. "The statements we have called stereotypes in the past have become true."[4]

Over the past two decades, the nation has seen this dichotomy grow, creating, in essence, two black Americas.

THE LOWER ECHELON

- Proportion of black families in the nonworking poor:
  - In 1969: 14 percent
  - In 1986: 30 percent[5]
- Proportion of black children now born out of wedlock:
  - Three in five[6]
- Proportion of black male high school dropouts who did not work in the past year:
  - In 1973: 15 percent
  - In 1986: 40 percent[7]

THE UPPER ECHELON

- Percentage of black families in the upper class:
  - In 1969: 3 percent
  - In 1986: 9 percent[8]
- Percentage of black families in the middle class:
  - In 1969: 28 percent
  - In 1986: 38 percent[9]

FRUSTRATION

The media paints the state of race relations today as one of whites oppressing blacks, or of blacks resenting the white-dominated society. It paints two stark, opposing sides: liberals who are sympathetic to black concerns, and conservatives, who blame black people for their status in society.

More bluntly, the perception is something like this: whites hate blacks; blacks hate whites. One side berates "welfare queens," the other complains of "racist code words."

The truth isn't in the extremes. The truth is something more complex. If you listen, you don't hear hate; you hear frustration. "I don't mind helping," says a working-class white carpenter, "but somebody has got to help themselves, you've got to pull. When you try to pick somebody up, they have to help."[10]

THREE CHOICES

The disparity between the races isn't a simple, polarizing issue. And most Americans aren't vilifying each other. They're struggling to make sense of it, to find a way to make things better.

We agree on the goal of racial parity and harmony. But we disagree on how to get there. The disparities center on three issues:

- *Past or present?* Should we work to correct past wrongs as well as current differences—or simply work to have a just society in the present?
- *Government's role.* Should the government take a leadership role, or has too much government activity worked to *create* the black underclass?
- *Blacks or whites?* Are white Americans responsible for correcting wrongs and improving the plight of blacks, or must blacks take their fate into their own hands?

These are no small disagreements. They touch fundamental views of history, conceptions of government's role, and ideas about the responsibility of the individual and of society. Clearly, though, they are disagreements that recognize the complexity of the issue.

Rather than accentuating the differences, we sought the middle ground. Rather than further polarize, we wanted to see where we agree, where there's consensus.

☆

Judge us by our character, not our color.

That message comes through from all segments of the American populace. There's agreement: Virtually all Americans—black and white—agree on the ideal of a color-blind society.

That ideal aside, we asked:

- Is that ideal a reality?
- Do blacks and whites mix socially?
- Do racist attitudes persist?

The answers were sobering:

- Racial resentment and misperceptions persist.
- Blacks and whites retain social distance.
- At the extremes, racism persists.

THE EXTREMES AND THE CENTER

On one side, we found racism; on the other side, a call for government action; and in the middle we found most Americans.

RACISM

- *19 percent* of Americans hold hard-core racist attitudes.

GOVERNMENT ACTION

- *13 percent* of Americans say the government should take an active role in correcting past racial wrongs in the workplace, education, and politics.

THE CENTER

- *68 percent* of Americans are in neither camp.

THE COLOR-BLIND CONSENSUS _____

Considering that institutionalized racism was brought to an end just three decades ago, it's incredible to consider the progress: the large majority of blacks and whites support the notion that we ought to function and interact without regard to the color of our skin.

RIGHTS AND RESPONSIBILITIES

- *97 percent* of Americans say all races should share equal benefits, privileges, and responsibilities of citizenship.

CHARACTER

- *96 percent* say the best society is color-blind—judging based on talents, merits, and accomplishments.

LAWS

- *90 percent* say all Americans—regardless of race, color, or creed— are equal under the law.

AN ATTACK ON GOVERNMENT QUOTAS? _____

Is there anything wrong with calling for total equality, regardless of race? Perhaps.

Why? Because it hasn't always been that way. Admittedly, the nation has a history of slavery, segregation, and built-in racism. The argument of many black Americans says: Attitudes are helpful, but *they won't change society.* They won't make whites hire blacks, they won't make the schools equally good, they won't integrate the neighborhoods. Only laws will change society.

But white Americans overwhelmingly reject the idea of racial quotas— or any government action to correct racial inequities:

EQUALITY

- *95 percent* say it's wrong to treat different races differently to correct past failures.

JOBS

- *96 percent* oppose instituting racial or ethnic quotas in hiring and promotion.

UNIVERSITIES

- *95 percent* oppose racial or ethnic quotas in college admissions and hiring of faculty.

REACHING THE GOAL

- *Only 35 percent* say we can never become fully "color-blind" unless we first undo the damage of the past.

Clearly, the majority of white Americans feel that government intervention in these matters hinders progress, rather than fostering racial harmony.

Why? Today, almost nobody in America would argue that black Americans should be denied education, or the rewards of employment and success in the wider society. Affirmative Action and similar quota policies, however, have not achieved their purpose; rather, they've served to further divide the nation by fostering resentment and feelings of injustice. Clearly, Americans believe that the best way to eliminate all racial barriers is to eliminate *any* policies that treat races differently.

WHO'S RESPONSIBLE?

If racial quotas aren't the tool, how will equality be achieved?

More and more, white Americans are coming to believe that blacks should take responsibility for their own futures, rather than focusing on the wrongs of the past or counting on government intervention.

Accountability. We asked white Americans: Who has the greatest responsibility for ensuring that blacks succeed and share in the American dream?

- Government: 5 percent
- Whites: 16 percent
- Blacks: 88 percent

Clearly, white Americans—who share with blacks the goal of a color-blind society—are frustrated with the lack of progress. But they put the blame on the shoulders of blacks.

RACE AND SOCIAL DISTANCE

The ideal is one matter.

Reality is another.

Our value system places an emphasis on being blind to skin color. Are we?

No. White Americans continue to hold views that keep the races separate and distant in social actions large and small.

"THERE GOES THE NEIGHBORHOOD"

- *53 percent* of Americans say their neighbors would have objections to blacks moving into the neighborhood.

RACIAL DETOURS

- *31 percent* say that when driving they sometimes detour to avoid a "predominantly black" section of town.

EDUCATION

- *53 percent* would have qualms about sending their kids to a predominantly black school.

FRIENDS

- *72 percent* of whites say only a few of their closest friends are not white.

LOVE

- *53 percent* say they could never get romantically involved with someone of another race.
- *52 percent* would object if their child married someone of another race.

Clearly, when it comes to issues of race, the ideals that Americans state in abstract terms stand in contradiction to the personal attitudes most white Americans hold more privately.

RACISM

We agree, then, that our society ought not to judge people based on their ethnicity, their skin color—any factor beyond their control.

We agree that we shouldn't. But many of us do.

It's difficult to reconcile, but it's true: age-old racial stereotypes persist—even in a society where everyone agrees that we all ought to be equal.

THE WORK ETHIC

- *77 percent* of Americans say some racial and ethnic groups work harder than others to get ahead.
- *28 percent* of whites say the races have the same opportunities, but blacks lack the ability, drive, and willpower to succeed.

AMBITION

- *43 percent* of whites say that blacks have less motivation and willpower than whites.

BRAIN POWER AND DRIVE

- *34 percent* of whites say some races are more intelligent and work harder than others.

A UNITY OF PURPOSE

What Americans say about race reveals a conflict between the internal and the external, between goals and reality. Certainly, the social distance between the races and the widespread nature of racist attitudes is disturbing. But we choose not to emphasize that. We choose to place our hope not in what separates us, but what draws us together.

A *nearly unanimous* majority of Americans share the goals of equality and equal opportunity. Much needs to be done to reach that goal, but we place our hope in common aspiration.

GUN CONTROL

Progun. Antigun. And nothing in between.

So goes the myth that has shaped up over decades in America. We're a nation divided between those who would arm themselves to the teeth and those who want to disarm even duck hunters.

Conservatives want their guns. Liberals want to get rid of them. Or do they? Is the nation divided over the gun problem? We were surprised to learn the truth.

The debate falls along unambiguous lines. But how much do Americans split themselves into those camps?

THE BATTLE

The gun control debate is clear and well defined:

POINT _____

Handguns are a societal menace and should not be available to the general public.

—Michael Beard, President, Coalition to Stop Gun Violence

COUNTERPOINT _____

A lot that is theoretical, ideological, is being written by people who have not been threatened, have not had a stranger at the bedroom window at 2 A.M. and have not been confronted by a doped-up intruder just outside their door.

—Columnist Carl Rowan, on why he shot at trespassers on his property

JUST THE FACTS

Before we review the debate, we'll start with a few facts.

The law. Under federal law, anyone over twenty-one who doesn't have a criminal record or a history of mental illness can purchase a handgun. (Anyone over eighteen, a shotgun or rifle.) But the law restricting people with criminal pasts and the mentally ill is routinely ignored.

The numbers. About two in five Americans have firearms in their homes.[1] How many guns do Americans own?[2]

- Total: over 300 million
- Handguns: 60 million
- Shotguns and rifles: 140 million
- Semiautomatic assault weapons: 1 million

Handguns. Every two years, as many Americans are killed by handguns as were killed in the Vietnam War—nearly 25,000 annually.[3]

- 12,000 die annually in handgun-related suicides.[4]
- 1,000 die annually in unintentional handgun shootings.[5]

CEASE-FIRE: THE CASE AGAINST GUNS

The death toll. Is it important to have a gun to protect yourself? Perhaps it helps. But the real picture is startling: your gun is more likely to kill someone you know than an intruder.

- Handguns kept at home are forty-three times likelier to kill the gun's owner, friend, or relative than to kill an intruder.[6]
- More handgun homicide victims die in arguments than in felony-related incidents.[7]
- Of the 11,700 handgun-related homicides in 1990, only 215 were ruled justifiable.

Crime. An armed population is hurting crime prevention more than aiding police. Three in four police killed in the line of duty are killed with handguns.[8]

Cost. Guns cost the nation billions in medical costs and lost productivity.

- Total annual cost of U.S. firearm injuries: $14.4 billion
- Total annual hospital costs for treating gunshot victims: $1 billion[9]

America and the world. The United States has far more guns than any other nation; most developed nations have virtual bans on handguns. The results? The nation's homicide rate is

- 11 times Great Britain's
- 9 times Japan's
- 8.5 times Germany's[10]

Among men aged fifteen to twenty-four, the U.S. homicide rate is

- 44 times Japan's
- 22 times Germany's
- 18 times Great Britain's[11]

Out of control. In fact, there are so many guns that violence is spiraling out of control. Many large cities annually set new records for homicides.

- *Homicide.* In 1990 and 1991, these cities all broke their all-time homicide records: San Diego, Dallas, Phoenix, Los Angeles, New York, Boston, Charlotte, Milwaukee, Oakland, Colorado Springs, Minneapolis, Rochester, New Orleans, and Columbus.[12]
- *Children.* Gunshot wounds among children in urban areas nearly doubled between 1987 and 1990.

READY, AIM: THE CASE FOR GUNS

Self-defense. As our society becomes increasingly violent and dangerous, it's more difficult to rely on police for protection. Gun-control opponents argue that the best way to protect yourself from criminals is with a gun.

- *Intent.* Nearly three in five legal handgun owners buy them for self-defense.[13]

- *Use.* Handguns are used for self-defense 645,000 times annually.
- *Rape prevention.* Using a gun for protection reduces the likelihood of a completed rape.
- *Aiding police.* Armed citizens kill two to seven times the number of criminals killed each year by law enforcement.[14]

Tough on crime. Several studies of criminal activity show that criminals tend to act based on whether their potential victims might be armed.

- *Crime prevention.* More than half of "handgun predators" did not commit at least one crime for fear the victim was armed.[15]
- *Avoiding guns.* Three in four criminals said burglars avoid dwellings where they fear being shot.
- *The fear factor.* Three in five criminals said they fear being shot by citizens more than by police.[16]

Control and crime. Does gun control prevent crime? Ironically, the cities with the strictest gun-control laws have the most gun violence, and those with the most lenient laws have the lowest rates of homicide and robbery.

- *Washington, D.C.* The nation's capital has a virtual handgun ban. Yet between 1976 and 1991, murder tripled, and handgun-related crimes quadrupled.
- *New York.* Since New York enforced a virtual ban on handguns, the city's homicide rate has risen three times faster than the nation's.[17]

America and the world. Do guns cause crime? Perhaps not. U.S. crime rates—compared to Europe's and Japan's—are even higher in classes of crimes where guns are rarely used, such as rape and robbery.

Moreover, since Great Britain adopted its strict antigun laws, its murder rate has doubled.[18]

THE SECOND AMENDMENT

"A well regulated Militia, being necessary to the security of a free State, the right of the people to keep and bear Arms, shall not be infringed."

The Second Amendment to the United States Constitution is engraved on the building housing the National Rifle Association, the powerful national gun lobby. Yet its meaning and intent is open to interpretation.

The question: Whose right is it? The individual's? Or the states'?

A collective right. Several court decisions indicate that the amendment doesn't guarantee individuals the right to have guns—one significant ruling found that the amendment "guarantees a collective rather than an individual right."[19]

Retired Chief Justice Warren E. Burger has stated that "the need for a state militia was the predicate of the 'right' guarantee."

In fact, the Supreme Court has upheld several lower-court decisions banning or limiting whole categories of weapons, including sawed-off shotguns and machine guns.

Writes Erin Griswald, former dean of the Harvard Law School:

> Indeed, that the Second Amendment poses no barrier to strong gun laws is perhaps the most well-settled proposition in United States Constitutional Law.[20]

An individual right. Yet to opponents of gun control, the Second Amendment speaks for itself. They argue that the "collective right" interpretation is a twentieth-century invention. The framers of the Constitution, they note, always used the word "right" to apply to individuals, and always mentioned "states" to imply a collective meaning.

Further, the NRA asserts: "All four relevant Supreme Court decisions have recognized that the Second Amendment guarantees an individual right to keep and bear arms. No Supreme Court decision has ever held this right to be collective."[21]

☆

The argument has raged for years. The sides are clear. The question: Is America truly divided over guns?

Though gun control has been portrayed consistently as a divisive issue, Americans are of a clear and unified mind. In almost every category, the majority agree on the direction the nation should take: the majority of Americans support gun control.

- *Brady Bill.* Eighty-eight percent support laws to require a waiting period before one can purchase a handgun.
- *Pinning the blame.* Ninety-one percent support making gun manufacturers and/or licensing authorities liable for violence and damage caused by guns they helped put in circulation.
- *Punishment.* Eighty-two percent say individuals in illegal possession of guns should face mandatory jail terms.

CURTAILING A RIGHT

The clearest sign of Americans' feelings about the nation's proliferation of guns is their reaction to the Second Amendment. *Eighty-four percent* of Americans want to repeal the Second Amendment—the right to bear arms.

PROGUN

Why do some Americans oppose gun control? We learned from the 16 percent of people who oppose revoking the constitutional right to own arms.

INEFFECTIVE

- *97 percent* said gun control wouldn't reduce crime.
- *93 percent* said gun control wouldn't reduce homicide.

INSECURE

- *78 percent* said they'd sleep better with a gun in the house.

INSIDE THE PROGUN MENTALITY

Even among the ranks of the hard-core progun population—those who favor keeping the Second Amendment—we found support for gun control.

- *Punishment.* Eighty percent say illegal possession of guns should lead to mandatory jail sentences.
- *Security.* Forty percent say they would sleep better knowing criminals didn't have easy access to guns.
- *Waiting period.* Thirty-seven percent support requiring anyone seeking to buy a gun to wait—so their criminal and psychological records can be checked.
- *Assault rifles.* Thirty-three percent support banning semiautomatic assault rifles.
- *Control.* Ten percent support strict gun-control regulation in order to reduce violent crime in our cities.

WHY NO PROGRESS?

With such a clear mandate, why haven't we taken more action? The NRA remains one of the wealthiest and most powerful lobbies in Washington. Though clearly representing a minority of Americans, it exerts massive clout. The association and its political action committee, the Political Victory Fund, have spent about $8.4 million in political donations. The organizations claim a victory rate of about 82 percent.

U.S. VS. NRA

In the end, it appears the nation *is* clearly divided over gun control—but not the way Americans have come to believe. It's not an even playing field. It's a battle of lobbyists versus citizens, of money versus beliefs. It's the debate of a well-funded minority facing up to the opinion of the majority.

- *D.C. clout.* Thirty-six percent of the progun sample agree that the government's lack of action on gun control shows how influential the NRA and other lobbies are.

TAKING CONTROL

Clearly, gun control is an issue the people need to take back into their own hands—away from the politicians, away from the lobbyists, away from the media.

ABORTION

Look for strife and you'll find it. Look for division, for enmity, for disagreement, and it'll be there.

But look for consensus . . . and you may be surprised. We were.

Since the Supreme Court made abortion legal with the 1973 *Roe* v. *Wade* decision, abortion has become a touchstone, a rallying point, the center of an insoluble debate. Witness the extremes:

> It is a fundamental constitutional liberty that individual Americans—not government—can best take responsibility for making the most difficult and intensely personal decisions regarding reproduction.
>
> —*1992 Democratic Party Platform*

> We believe the unborn child has a fundamental right to life which cannot be infringed.
>
> —*1992 Republican Party Platform*

America is divided.

Or is it?

It's become an accepted part of contemporary America that abortion is tearing the nation apart. Pro-life. Pro-choice. (For simplicity, we'll use those politically loaded terms.) Fundamentalist fanatics. Baby killers. The abortion debate is an open wound, a festering, painful conflict that—most of us have come to believe—can never be settled.

It just runs too deep. Beliefs. Religion. Freedom. Privacy. The conventional wisdom says that feelings are so deep that they simply can't be changed. That America must come to live with the strife.

When we listened to Americans, we found something quite different. Certainly, there are extremes. But also, Americans articulated common feelings, shared beliefs, and seldom expressed ambivalence. Within the struggle, we found cause for hope.

249

THE FACTS

Before we delve into the controversy, it's important to understand the facts: What is the state of abortion in America today?

Numbers. Between 1973—when abortion became legal—and 1992, doctors performed 28 million abortions in America—about 1.6 million per year.[1]

- *Three of ten pregnancies.* Thirty percent of all U.S. pregnancies end in abortion—half the unwanted pregnancies.[2]
- *Three in one hundred women.* Three percent of all women of child-bearing age have an abortion each year.
- *Second abortions.* More than four in ten women receiving an abortion have had one before.
- *Birth control.* Only 9 percent of women having abortions have ever used birth control.[3]

Pre-Roe. Before legalization, in the 1960s, more than *one million* illegal abortions were done annually. More than 350,000 women annually suffered medical complications from abortion serious enough to warrant hospitalization.

The world leader. More abortions are performed in America than in any other developed nation. The United States also has the highest rate of pregnancies ending in abortion. How many pregnancies are aborted?[4]

- United States: 30 percent
- Japan: 26 percent
- Australia: 20 percent
- United Kingdom: 19 percent
- The Netherlands: 9 percent

The powerless. The women who are most likely to seek abortions are those with the least power in society—the young, the poor, the unwed, the members of minority groups.

- *Single.* Unmarried women are *five times* more likely to seek abortions to terminate unwanted pregnancies.

- *Poor.* Poor women are *three times* more likely to undergo abortions than wealthier women.
- *Minority.* Nonwhite women are *three times* more likely than white women to get abortions.[5]

Teens. Nearly two-thirds of American teenagers are sexually active—and 84 percent of U.S. women have had sexual intercourse by age twenty.[6] So it's no surprise that so many teenage women seek abortions.

- *One in four abortions.* Teenage women get 416,000 abortions annually—26 percent of all abortions.
- *Unwanted pregnancies.* More than eight of ten teenage pregnancies are unwanted—and 41 percent of these end in abortion.[7]

Despite sex education in the schools and widespread public education programs, more than *one in four* teenagers receiving abortions have never used birth control.

Religion's impact. Women with strong religious affiliations are less likely to seek abortions.

- *Christians.* "Born Again" Christians are half as likely as the national average to seek abortions.
- *Protestants and Jews.* Women who identify themselves as Protestants and Jews are the least likely to obtain abortions.
- *Catholics.* Among Catholic women, the abortion rate is identical to the national average.[8]

Rape and incest. It's relatively rare for women to seek abortion as a result of incest or rape. Only about one in one thousand U.S. abortions are performed on women impregnated during acts of rape or incest.

Timing. Women tend to have abortions early in their pregnancies. Nearly *nine in ten* abortions take place in the first trimester of a pregnancy.[9]

- First 8 weeks: 50 percent
- 9–10 weeks: 27 percent
- 11–12 weeks: 12 percent
- 13–15 weeks: 6 percent

- 16–20 weeks: 4 percent
- 21 or more weeks: less than 1 percent

Safety. Abortion has become a very safe procedure for the mother. In fact, childbirth is *eleven times* more likely than abortion to lead to the mother's death.

Government funding. Since 1977, the United States has barred the use of federal funds to pay for abortions for Medicaid-eligible women (except when the mother's life is in danger).

A LOOK AT THE EXTREMES

For all appearances, it looks like a war.

On both sides of the abortion debate, there are extremes: violence, extreme rhetoric, anger, fear.

The best way to understand the depth of emotion and anger that dominate the debate is to witness a face-to-face confrontation between a pro-life activist and a pro-choice activist. Journalist Roger Rosenblatt describes one:

The pro-lifer: "His face was pulled tight about the jaw, which thrust forward like a snowplow attachment on the grille of a truck. From the flattened O of his mouth, the word 'murderer' erupted in a regular rhythm, the repetition of the *r*'s giving the word the sound of an outboard motor that failed to catch."

The pro-choicer: "She, for her part, paced up and down directly in front of him, saying nothing. Instead, she held high a large cardboard sign on a stick, showing the cartoonish drawing of a bloody coat hanger over the caption, 'Never Again.' Like his, her face was taut with fury, her lips pressed together so tightly they folded under and vanished. Whenever she drew close to him, she would deliberately lower the sign and turn it toward him, so that he would be yelling his 'murderer' at the picture of the coat hanger."[10]

The extremes play themselves out in grisly scenarios.

Murder. On the morning of March 10, 1993, Dr. David Gunn pulled up to the rear entrance of the Florida clinic where he performed abortions. As he got out of his car, Michael F. Griffin, a thirty-one-year-old right-to-life activist, approached him and shot him three times in the back.

Gunn's murder (Griffin confessed immediately) was only the most extreme result of a movement that has been marked by violence. Since 1984, there have been more than 1,000 reports of violence against abortion providers—186 in 1992 alone.[11] Most pro-life activists abhor these incidents, but they reflect the debate's level of intensity and emotion.

Suicide? The emotions run as deep among those who support the right to abortion. One twenty-one-year-old woman who received an abortion was asked what she would have done if she hadn't had that option.

"I don't know," she said. "Perhaps suicide. I do know though if abortion is illegal any doctor is welcome to perform safe abortions at my house. I won't let girls stick hangers up them."[12]

THE ABORTION QUESTION

It's easy to see the conflict. We sought the common ground. We wanted to see what Americans share. We asked:

- Do pro-choice Americans hold pro-life values?
- Do all pro-choice people advocate abortion if parents are simply unhappy with the sex of the fetus?
- Do pro-lifers believe women should be compelled to give birth to deformed babies?
- What about rape or incest?
- How do people on both sides feel about forcing women who habitually get pregnant to be sterilized?
- Should the government pay for abortions?

☆	**THE PEOPLE SPEAK. . .**	☆
	ON ABORTION	

THE ANSWERS

First, we looked at the picture using the traditional framework—the one that assumes the nation is split in two. We started by asking Americans to respond to the statement:

"An abortion should be available on demand to all women who want one."

The result:

- *Pro-choice:* 58 percent agreed
- *Pro-life:* 42 percent disagreed

The simplistic, shallow analysis: The nation is divided into two irreconcilable groups. We think that assessment underestimates the complexity and depth of Americans.

A SPECTRUM OF EMOTION

The truth: We're conflicted, confused, and uncertain. The true abortion discussion doesn't take place in straightforward black-and-white terms. Opinions don't come at the extremes, they're along a continuum.

PRO-LIFE

Are all Americans who identify with the pro-life side of the debate extremist ideologues screaming "Murder!" in front of abortion clinics?

In brief: No.

When asked to apply theoretical situations to real life, the majority of those who identify with the pro-life side are much softer on the issue.

254

HOW DO "PRO-LIFERS" FEEL ABOUT ABORTION?

- Abortion is *not* murder: 67 percent
- The Constitution should *not* be amended to outlaw abortion: 57 percent
- The decision on abortion is up to the mother: 17 percent

HOW MANY "PRO-LIFERS" SAY ABORTION SHOULD BE ALLOWED. . .

- If the mother's life is in danger: 62 percent
- In case of rape or incest: 55 percent
- If there is a strong chance that the baby would be born retarded, deformed, or otherwise handicapped: 53 percent
- If the mother feels she isn't ready to have children: 10 percent

PRO-CHOICE

What does it mean to favor abortion on demand? Do most pro-choice supporters advocate abortion without giving a thought to the fetus, without considering the complex issues involved in the decision to terminate a pregnancy?

No. In fact, many Americans who support the principle of abortion are ambivalent enough about their stance that they favor putting limitations and conditions on its practice.

SHOULD THERE BE RESTRICTIONS?

- Stricter limits than are now in place should be adopted: 11 percent

SHOULD THE GOVERNMENT PAY?

- The government should not fund abortions: 57 percent

WHOSE DECISION IS IT?

- The father should have some legal say in whether an abortion can be performed: 53 percent

- A woman should not get an abortion without the consent of her husband: 27 percent
- Young girls should not be able to get abortions without their parents' permission: 51 percent

WHAT MOTIVATIONS ARE JUSTIFIED?

- A woman's not feeling "ready" to have a child isn't reason enough to allow an abortion: 19 percent
- A woman's feeling that she is too poor to take care of the child isn't reason enough: 18 percent

SHARING THE MIDDLE GROUND

Clearly, the popular picture of a nation divided into pro-choicers and pro-lifers isn't a reality. The extremes certainly exist:

- *The pro-choice extreme:* How many Americans support abortion on demand *and* federal funding for abortion? 17 percent.
- *The pro-life extreme:* How many Americans say abortion is murder and support a constitutional amendment to outlaw it? 11.7 percent.

The conclusion: 29 percent of Americans find themselves on the extremes. Which means that *71 percent*—more than two-thirds of the nation—is somewhere in the middle on the issue. The majority of Americans share the middle ground.

Is America torn apart by abortion? Yes. But the confusion and conflict is greater *in our own hearts* than on the protest lines or on the evening news. We're disturbed and ambivalent. But we understand the complexity of the issue.

Abortion is the most vexing moral issue of our time. What many Americans share in common is that internal debate—the feeling that this is morally ambivalent, yet the government ought not make the decision.

SEXUAL DISCRIMINATION AND HARASSMENT

He said. She said. Whom do you believe?

It comes down to that.

Clarence Thomas and Anita Hill. An executive and his secretary. A professor and his student.

He said. She said. Whom do you believe?

Is the nation divided: men against women? Are we headed for an era of strife between the sexes? We asked for the truth—and we found out.

Sexual harassment wasn't talked about much until a week in the fall of 1991 when the nation sat at its television sets and watched the spectacle of Judge Clarence Thomas's Supreme Court confirmation hearing. Did he sexually harass Anita Hill when he was her boss, years before?

The issue riveted the nation—not only because of its dramatic value, its moment-to-moment intensity, but because it was a touchstone for our national consciousness. It caught the nation in the midst of a changing view of itself.

No matter which side you believe, it made you ask:

- "What is sexual harassment, anyway?"
- "If what he did was wrong, then what about what I did?"
- "If she was harassed, maybe I was too."

MIXED REACTION

In the immediate wake of the hearings, it was clear that the nation was already divided on the issue. The fact: Men and women have different ideas about what constitutes sexual harassment—and who can be believed.

Treatment. Percentage of Americans who said the Senate committee had treated Hill unfairly:

- 1991: 8 percent
- 1992: 39 percent

Women. Percentage of women who believed Hill's story:

- 1991: 24 percent
- 1992: 48 percent

Men. Percentage of men who believed Thomas's story:

- 1991: 69 percent
- 1992: 44 percent

Confirmation. Percentage of women who supported Thomas's Supreme Court nomination:

- 1991: 58 percent
- 1992: 44 percent

DEFINING THE TERMS

This much is certain: Americans don't really know what sexual harassment is.

A definition:

> Unwelcome sexual conduct in the work place, including pressure for dates or sexual favors, explicit sexual remarks, derogatory or suggestive gestures, leering or ogling, touching, or even actual or attempted assault or rape.[1]

Legal basis. The legal underpinnings of sexual harassment laws were put forth by the Supreme Court in its decision in *Meritor Savings* v. *Vinson,* in which it said that Title VII of the Civil Rights Act of 1964 "affords employees the right to work in an environment free from discriminatory intimidation, ridicule and insult."[2]

Unwelcome conduct. According to Chief Justice William Rehnquist, the key question is whether sexual behavior is "unwelcome conduct"—

whether or not the victim continued to engage in a relationship with the harasser.[3]

Verbal harassment. Physical harassment need not be an element of a claim of sexual harassment, lower court rulings have found; verbal harassment is sufficient.[4]

HOW COMMON?

As a major issue, it's fairly new. But sexual harassment has been around for a long time.

- *Two in three.* Nearly two-thirds of working women report having been sexually harassed.[5]
- *More charges.* Between 1988 and 1992, the number of individuals filing sexual harassment charges doubled:[6]
  - In 1988: 5,499
  - In 1992: 10,532

In a 1988 study, *42 percent* of women working in the federal government said they had been victims of sexual harassment.[7]

Unreported. Yet the practice is seldom brought to the attention of authorities. According to the same 1988 study, only five in one hundred women filed formal complaints.[8]

THE COSTS

In addition to the moral and social toll, sexual harassment takes a financial toll. The incidents cost the typical *Fortune* 500 company $6.7 million annually as a result of employees missing work, employee turnover, low morale, and low productivity brought about by sexual harassment.[9]

THE PEOPLE SPEAK...

☆   ☆

ON SEXUAL DISCRIMINATION AND HARASSMENT

☆

There's a consensus in America: Society discriminates against women. What is striking is how people's opinions on that very issue are the best markers of the gaps that exist between the sexes.

On nearly every issue regarding relations between the sexes—the workplace, child care, harassment—men and women differ.

DISCRIMINATION

- *81 percent* of Americans say sexual discrimination against women has not been eliminated.
  - Men: 63 percent
  - Women: 82 percent
  - The gap: *19 percent* more women
- *71 percent* of Americans say discrimination exists—but less than in the past.
  - Men: 86 percent
  - Women: 61 percent
  - The gap: *25 percent* more men
- *46 percent* of Americans say sex discrimination is commonplace in America.
  - Men: 35 percent
  - Women: 53 percent
  - The gap: *18 percent* more women

THE WORKPLACE

- *81 percent* of Americans say women still don't get equal pay for equal work.

- Men: 74 percent
- Women: 85 percent
- The gap: *11 percent* more women
- *69 percent* of Americans say most corporations still pass over women for promotions.
  - Men: 58 percent
  - Women: 76 percent
  - The gap: *18 percent* more women

HARASSMENT

- *53 percent* say that until men and women have equal rights in the workplace, women will continue to be sexually harassed by men.
  - Men: 34 percent
  - Women: 64 percent
  - The gap: *30 percent* more women
- *57 percent* of Americans say more laws must be passed to protect women from sexual harassment in the workplace.
  - Men: 32 percent
  - Women: 73 percent
  - The gap: *41 percent* more women

WHAT IS SEXUAL HARASSMENT?

Sexual harassment is not the same as rape. It is more subtle, in a grayer area. As its occurrence has become more and more openly discussed, a definition has remained elusive. What, exactly, has to happen between two people to qualify as sexual harassment? Does it have to be physical? Or are words enough?

CONTACT

93 percent of Americans say there doesn't have to be physical contact to make a situation sexual harassment.

COERCION

71 percent of Americans say there doesn't have to be physical coercion or intimidation to make a situation sexual harassment.

SEXUAL HARASSMENT: CASE BY CASE

One of the myths about sexual harassment is that women tend to misinterpret innocent exchanges and comments—or genuine sexual attraction—and label it harassment.

That's not what we found.

Perhaps the relative novelty of the issue and the growing media attention it has received have blurred the lines and made some Americans hypersensitive to the problem.

In fact, men are more prone than women to label a situation sexual harassment. In almost every case we considered, men were *more likely* than women to cry: "Harassment!"

Consider a male supervisor and his female subordinate. The question: Is it sexual harassment if he repeatedly

	Men	Women	The Gap
asks her to have sex?	93%	96%	3% fewer men
discusses pornography with her?	84%	90%	6% fewer men
tells her jokes with sexual references?	72%	69%	3% more men
puts his arm around her shoulders or back?	73%	67%	6% more men
pressures her to go out to dinner?	73%	67%	6% more men
asks her for a date?	46%	45%	1% more men
flirts with her?	32%	25%	7% more men

Consider two coworkers, a male and a female. The question: Is it sexual harassment if he repeatedly

	Men	Women	The Gap
asks her to have sex?	88%	83%	5% more men
tells her jokes with sexual references?	61%	54%	7% more men
puts his arm around her shoulders or back?	64%	51%	13% more men
pressures her to go out to dinner?	56%	42%	14% more men
asks her out on a date?	26%	18%	8% more men

PUNISHING HARASSERS

What sort of punishment is appropriate for sexual harassment? Americans seem to favor leniency over swift and extreme action.

Question: What's the best way to deal with a man who sexually harasses a woman on the job?

	Men	Women	The Gap
Give him a chance to explain his actions and change his behavior—without losing his job.	90%	78%	12% more men
Give him a warning the first time, but fire him if he harasses again.	83%	79%	4% more men
Fire him immediately.	8%	18%	10% fewer men

WHOSE FAULT IS IT?

The question persists: Do women bring harassment on themselves? Are there forms of behavior that encourage men to act in ways that are labeled as harassment?

Men are more likely than women to blame women's behavior, dress, and manner for bringing on the harassment.

	Men	Women	The Gap
Looks A woman's attractiveness or mode of dress can never be an excuse for sexual harassment.	61%	70%	9% fewer men
Dress A woman who wears sexy outfits to work has only herself to blame if she gets sexually harassed. Do you *disagree*?	57%	60%	3% fewer men
Flirting A woman flirting with a man in the workplace has only herself to blame if she gets sexually harassed by someone. Do you *disagree*?	51%	61%	10% fewer men

Blame

In all sexual harassment situations, both the man and woman are to be blamed equally.	15%	12%	3% more men
In all sexual harassment situations, only the man is guilty and the woman is simply the innocent victim.	1%	13%	12% fewer men

AN ELUSIVE DEFINITION

We agree to oppose it. But we don't agree what it is.

The fact is, society has changed: Some actions that might now be perceived as sexual harassment were, a few decades ago, routine, accepted behavior. So who makes the rules?

Some forms of harassment are so blatant that everyone agrees they're wrong. But what about the way we use language? What about innuendo? When it comes to those more subtle varieties of harassment, the sexes still seem divided. Men and women seem to be looking through different lenses.

Yet there's hope for reconciliation. Society changes and evolves. As the Hill-Thomas hearings showed, we are constantly changing our perceptions about what's acceptable and what's not. Over time, as those rules become clearer and more public, the divisions may well fade away.

WHAT HAPPENS NOW?

We can wait. We can do nothing. We can bury our heads in the sand. And America will continue to decay.

- The deficit will plunge us into ever-increasing debt.
- Drugs, crime, and guns will make our cities unlivable war zones.
- The crumbling education system will render us an illiterate, backward nation.
- An inequitable health-care system will ensure that growing numbers of people go without basic medical aid.

We can wait. And we can watch America slip away. We can watch hope fade into oblivion.

We can wait.

And it will be too late.

NO TIME TO LOSE

Of course, we can't really wait. As we listened to Americans, they told us: there's simply no time to waste.

The issues the American people have raised in this book—from drugs to education to the mounting deficit—are urgent. These aren't just topics for heady intellectual debate. A few more years of delay and inattention and denial will ruin us.

These ailments are destroying America. They're killing us. They're stealing our children's future. They're taking away our hope.

When we stopped to listen, the people said it time and time again: There's no choice. We've got to act now—before it's too late.

BRING ON THE REVOLUTION

The revolution has begun.

The signs are all around: Americans are fed up with the status quo. They're coming to sense that the traditional institutions—the political parties, the Congress, the White House—are failing them by sticking with politics as usual.

It's an era of crisis, and the government filibusters and procrastinates and studies and considers. Americans aren't content to wait for the sluggish process of party politics to get around to facing up to the pressing issues. The stakes are simply too high.

SIGNS OF DISCONTENT

Consider Ross Perot. Whatever his failings, the Texas billionaire had one significant accomplishment in the 1992 presidential race: he galvanized the huge numbers of Americans who feel disenfranchised, alienated, and downright angry about how government has failed them. His effort made it clear—beyond question—that Americans in huge numbers are willing to take action, to rethink politics, to reexamine the electoral process in order to seek solutions to the urgent problems around them.

RETHINKING AMERICA

The emergence of those dual factors—unprecedented crises and a populace eager for wholesale change—has created a fertile foundation for a revolution.

Are we calling for a radical overthrow of the government?

Not by any means.

Americans have faith—and a deep and abiding belief—in their national institutions. The discontent isn't with the structures of government, but rather with the way they've come to be used. Too many of us feel powerless next to large corporations, media conglomerates, and political parties.

The solution to the problems is not to abandon the government, nor to overthrow it.

It's to let it know how we feel. To make it represent us. And to make it work.

WHAT NOW?

Americans have spoken. We've identified the problems. And now we've come up with many of the solutions.

The beauty of American democracy is that it's a participatory system. We elect our representatives to represent *us*. Not their parties. Not their president. Not themselves. But us. Our role is to make sure they know what our agenda is—to communicate our urgent needs.

SIX ISSUES THAT MUST BE RESOLVED

The choice is to solve the problems—or slide into a tailspin.

Americans are clear about what must be done to restore America to strength and safety. These aren't ideological issues. They're not up for debate. Everyone agrees: Something must be done. Even if nothing else is addressed, these six crises must be cured—and the people are ready to act.

1. *Leaders who can lead.* It's time to put a new emphasis on bringing to the government people from all walks of life who embody the essential traits of the job: integrity, vision, and leadership capacity.
2. *A productive economy.* Americans value hard work and independence, and they want to give the supply-side approach a chance—to allow the people (and not the government) to restore the economy to strength.
3. *Schools that educate.* Parents are calling for more accountability of teachers and students; for more time in school; and for the option to choose where their children go to school.
4. *Health-care access for all.* Americans are united in their concern and fear for the millions among them who lack any insurance. They seek leadership that can unite them in solving the issue.

5. *Safer cities.* Sick of living in fear, Americans favor giving more power to police, granting courts more power over suspects, and building more prisons to confine criminals.
6. *A drug-free society.* It's time to crack down on drug dealers and users with tougher laws and wider drug testing.

THE TIME IS NOW

We can wait a year or two. Maybe three. But not much more. The problems are mounting. The crises are multiplying. The nation is crumbling. And we stand by and watch.

We've identified the problems.

We've chosen our solutions.

It's time to stop waiting.

Now it's time to act.

Now it's time to fix America.

A NOTE ON THE PROCESS

The research for this book was designed to address two substantive areas:

- The People's National Agenda: How to solve the nation's problems.
- The Quest for Leadership: What is leadership? Who fits the bill? Whom do the people choose?

THE PEOPLE'S NATIONAL AGENDA

The agenda emerged from four basic phases of research.

1. THE LOCAL TOWN HALL _____

Objective: To raise issues and discuss solutions.
 Method: Public forum.
 Details: We assembled one hundred Americans and asked them to debate the nation's issues, goals, and priorities; to explain why these issues are important; and to propose solutions.

2. THE SIMULATED NATIONAL TOWN HALL _____

Objective: To formulate a nationally projectable People's Agenda.
 Method: Telephone interviews.
 Details: We conducted one thousand telephone interviews among a nationally representative sampling of Americans. We asked them to expand on and quantify the National Agenda from the town-hall meeting. Each interview lasted approximately twenty minutes.
 The marginal error (statistical significance) for the univariate statistics reported in the book based on this survey can be inferred from the following table.

Margin of	Confidence Level				
Error for:	**95%**	**90%**	**85%**	**80%**	**75%**
N = 1000	±3.1%	±2.6%	±2.3%	±2.0%	±1.8%

3. THE QUEST FOR SOLUTIONS

Objective: To formulate solutions to the problems posed by the People's National Agenda.

Method: Interviews and study of literature.

Details: From our initial research and extensive secondary research—including interviews with policy experts and surveys of available literature from advocacy groups, think tanks, government agencies, and the popular media—we formulated proposals to solve the problems identified in our initial research.

4. THE SIMULATED NATIONAL REFERENDUM

Objective: To accurately gauge popular opinion regarding solutions to the problems cited in the People's National Agenda.

Method: Mail survey.

Details: Three thousand questionnaires were mailed to a nationally representative sampling of Americans (prerecruited by mail), with a cover letter explaining the nature and importance of the study and a one-dollar incentive for completing the questionnaire.

The questionnaire was in the form of a referendum, with proposed solutions to a range of issues. To reduce interview fatigue, questions were grouped into easy-to-digest segments. The questionnaire was designed to take about forty-five minutes to complete.

The following table lists question areas and the number of questions in each area.

Question Area   **Number of Questions**

Issues of Taxation and
   Funding for Federal Programs 95
Health Care .... 4 solutions*
The Economy .... 4 solutions
Education 14

*The word *solutions* denotes categories in which respondents were asked to choose one solution from a list of options.

A response rate of approximately 48.4 percent was realized, which resulted in a final sampling of 1,451.

The margin of error (statistical significance) for the univariate statistics reported in the book based on this survey can be inferred from the following table.

| Margin of | Confidence Level | | | | |
Error for:	95%	90%	85%	80%	75%
N = 1451	± 2.6%	± 2.2%	± 1.9%	± 1.7%	± 1.5%

THE QUEST FOR LEADERSHIP

The search for new national leadership proceeded in four phases:

1. THE LOCAL TOWN HALL _____

Objective: To survey opinion on leaders and leadership.

Method: Public forum.

Details: In the same town-hall meeting mentioned above, we gathered one hundred Americans and asked them to discuss leadership and specific national leaders. The discussion focused on five points.

- *Current national leaders.* How do they stack up?
- *Qualities.* What qualities, characteristics, and qualifications should be required for leaders?

- *Principles and signs.* What evidence do Americans use to determine whether their leaders are measuring up?
- *What we want.* What do Americans want their leaders to be and do? How much should they lead?
- *Who can lead?* Who (among current leaders) do Americans think has the capacity to lead the nation?

2. THE SIMULATED NATIONAL TOWN HALL _____

Objective: To develop specific criteria for leadership and potential candidates.

Method: Telephone survey.

Details: We conducted one thousand telephone interviews among a nationally representative sampling of Americans. We asked them to determine what kinds of men and women ought to lead the nation; to identify the character traits and qualifications they seek in their leaders. Each interview lasted approximately twenty minutes.

The marginal error (statistical significance) for the univariate statistics reported in the book based on this survey can be inferred from the following table.

Margin of Error for:	Confidence Level				
	95%	90%	85%	80%	75%
N = 1000	±3.1%	±2.6%	±2.3%	±2.0%	±1.8%

3. THE EXECUTIVE SEARCH _____

Objective: To find leadership candidates who meet the people's qualifications.

Method: Professional executive search process.

Details: We took the "leadership specs" developed in the first two phases of the process and turned them over to a prestigious national executive search firm. We asked the firm to create a list of candidates for the nation's top leadership posts.

The firm systematically searched and interviewed candidates, combing through the résumés of thousands of the most distinguished Americans of all political bents. Ultimately, a list of seven candidates was developed.

4. THE SIMULATED NATIONAL ELECTION _____

Objective: To choose a leader for America.

Method: Mail survey.

Details: Three thousand questionnaires were mailed to a representative sampling of Americans, with a cover letter explaining the nature and importance of the study, along with a one-dollar incentive for completing the questionnaire. Participants were asked to choose a candidate from a list of seven. Short biographies of the candidates were enclosed on cards, which were packed in the mail-out package in random order to avoid order bias in responses.

A response rate of 30.5 percent was realized, which resulted in a final sampling of 1,067.

The margin of error (statistical significance) for the univariate statistics reported in the book based on this survey can be inferred from the following table.

Margin of Error for:	Confidence Level				
	95%	**90%**	**85%**	**80%**	**75%**
N = 1,067	±3.0%	±2.5%	±2.2%	±2.0%	±1.8%

NOTES

PART I: WHO SHOULD LEAD US?

1. "Los Angeles Times Poll," *Los Angeles Times*, October 4–15, 1984.
2. "CBS/New York Times Poll," *The New York Times*, November 6, 1980.
3. The Roper Organization Inc., *Roper Reports 88–4* (New York: Roper Organization Inc., June 1988), p. 327.
4. Yankelovich, Skelly, and White, "Time/Yankelovich, Skelly and White," *Time*, April 28, 1976.
5. Yankelovich, Clancy, and Shulman, "Time/CNN/Yankelovich, Clancy and Shulman Poll," *Time*, August 19–20, 1992.
6. Virginia Slims, *1980 Virginia Slims Women's Survey*, conducted by The Roper Organization Inc. (Storrs, Conn.: 1980).
7. James Patterson and Peter Kim, *The Day America Told the Truth* (New York: Prentice Hall Press, 1991), p. 107.
8. "Barbara Jordan," *Gale Research*, Issue 1, November 1988.
9. Bonnie Angelo, "An Ethical Guru Monitors Morality," *Time*, June 3, 1991, p. 9.
10. "Barbara Jordan," *Gale Research*, Issue 1, November 1988.
11. Fred Barnes, "Kemp's Campaign," *USA Weekend*, August 16, 1992, p. 4.
12. "Ann Richards," *Current Biography Yearbook 1991*, p. 471.
13. "Ann Richards: Keynote Address at the Democratic National Convention, Atlanta, Ga.," *Vital Speeches*, August 15, 1988, p. 647.
14. "Ann Richards," *Current Biography Yearbook 1991*, p. 471.
15. Dick Youngblood, "Rudman Blames Bloated Federal Deficit on Electorate, Timid Politicians," *Minneapolis Star Tribune*, April 27, 1992, p.2D.
16. Nancy Traver, "Why Washington Doesn't Work," *Time*, April 6, 1992, pp. 20–21.
17. "Warren B. Rudman," *Current Biography Yearbook 1989*, p. 471.
18. Traver, "Why Washington Doesn't Work."
19. Susan Chira, "All Energy and Elbows: Donna Edna Shalala," *The New York Times*, December 12, 1992.
20. Cleveland Ceil, "Campus CEO," *Working Woman*, December 1991, p. 60.
21. Thomas A. Stewart, "Brainpower," *Fortune*, June 3, 1991, p. 44.
22. Susan Caminiti, "Payoff from a Good Reputation," *Fortune*, February 10, 1992, p. 74.
23. Ibid.

PART II

The Economy

1. Lester Thurow, *Head to Head* (New York: William Morrow, 1992), pp. 154–155.
2. Michael Wolff, *Where We Stand: Can America Make It in a Global Race for Wealth, Health and Happiness* (New York: Bantam Books, 1992), p. 24.
3. Thurow, *Head to Head*, p. 57.
4. Ibid., p. 155.
5. Council of Economic Advisors, "Economic Report to the President" (Washington, D.C.: U.S. Government Printing Office, 1991).
6. Thurow, *Head to Head*, p. 165.
7. Wolff, *Where We Stand*.
8. Ibid.
9. Thurow, *Head to Head*, pp. 155–156.
10. Robert B. Reich, *The Next American Frontier* (New York: Penguin Books, 1984), p. 117, and *The Work of Nations* (New York: Vintage Books, 1992), p. 76.
11. Reich, *The Next American Frontier*, p. 117.
12. Ibid., p. 122.
13. James Dale Davidson and Lord William Rees-Mogg, *The Great Reckoning* (New York: Summit Books, 1991), p. 102.
14. Ibid., p. 102.
15. "100 Largest Diversified Service Companies," *Fortune*, August 26, 1991, p. 171.
16. Gary Clyde Hufbauer, "Europe 1992: Opportunities and Challenges," *Brookings Review*, Vol. 8, No. 9 (Summer 1990), pp. 13–22.
17. Ibid.
18. Reich, *The Next American Frontier*, p. 118.
19. Thurow, *Head to Head*, p. 165.
20. Wolff, *Where We Stand*, p. 11.
21. Davidson and Rees-Mogg, *The Great Reckoning*, p. 108.
22. Wolff, *Where We Stand*, p. 13.
23. Ibid., p. 13.
24. Donald L. Bartlett and James B. Steele, *America: What Went Wrong* (Kansas City, Mo.: Andrews and McMeel, 1992), p. 4.
25. Ibid., p. 4.
26. Reich, *The Work of Nations*, p. 197.
27. Thurow, *Head to Head*, p. 164.
28. Reich, *The Work of Nations*, p. 197; Richard A. Musgrave, *Strengthening the Progressive Income Tax* (Washington, D.C.: Economic Policy Institute, 1989).
29. D. Elwood, *Poor Support: Poverty in the American Family* (New York: Basic Books, 1988).
30. Ibid.
31. Reich, *The Next American Frontier*, p. 207.
32. Ibid., p. 202.
33. Ibid., p. 208.

34. Thurow, *Head to Head,* p. 166.
35. Ibid., p. 157.
36. Leonard L. Lederman, "Science and Technology Policies and Priorities," *Science,* September 1987.
37. Thomas A. Stewart, "Where We Stand in the New American Century," *Fortune,* Special issue, 1991.
38. Thurow, *Head to Head,* p. 159.
39. Thomas D. Cabot, "Is American Education Competitive?," *Harvard Magazine,* Spring 1986.
40. Richard Peterson, *Adult Education Opportunities in the Nine Industrialized Countries* (Princeton N.J.: Educational Testing Service, September 1990), Vol. 1, pp. 98–147, 234–266.
41. Reich, *The Next American Frontier,* p. 220.
42. Ibid., pp. 220–221.
43. Ibid., pp. 121–122.
44. Ibid., p. 122.
45. Bartlett and Steele, *America: What Went Wrong,* p. 4.
46. Wolff, *Where We Stand,* p. 19.
47. Davidson and Rees-Mogg, *The Great Reckoning,* p. 97.
48. Ibid., p. 109.
49. Reich, *The Work of Nations,* pp. 243–244.
50. Reich, *The Next American Frontier,* p. 236.

Education

1. Wolff, *Where We Stand,* p. 55.
2. Ibid., p. 53.
3. Educational Testing Service, *Annual Report 1991* (Princeton, N.J.: ETS, 1991).
4. National Commission on Excellence in Education, *A Nation at Risk: A Full Account,* ed. U.S.A. Research Staff, 1983.
5. Stratford P. Sherman, "America Won't Win Till It Reads More," *The New York Times* (November 18, 1991), p. 201.
6. Ibid.
7. Davidson and Rees-Mogg, *The Great Reckoning,* p. 293.
8. William Celies III, "Study Says Half of Adults in the U.S. Lack Reading and Math Abilities," *The New York Times,* September 9, 1993, p. A1.
9. Ibid.
10. Reich, *The Next American Frontier,* p. 213.
11. Wolff, *Where We Stand,* p. 53.
12. Ibid., p. 51.
13. Ibid., p. 49.
14. Ibid., p. 50.
15. Cabot, "Is American Education Competitive?"
16. Thurow, *Head to Head,* p. 276.
17. "Public's Attitude Toward Public Schools," Gallup poll, 1991.
18. Troy Segal, "Saving Our Schools," *BusinessWeek,* September 14, 1992, p. 70.
19. Ibid.

20. "Public's Attitude Toward Public Schools."
21. Ibid.
22. U.S. National Center for Education Statistics, *Digest of Educational Statistics Annual 1991.*
23. Ibid.
24. Ibid.
25. M. B. Pearlstein, "Why the Schools Still Don't Work," *The Wilson Quarterly,* Summer 1991, pp. 88–89.
26. U.S. Department of Education, *Department of Education Annual Report 1991.*
27. Wolff, *Where We Stand,* p. 44.
28. Ibid., p. 47.
29. Ibid., p. 58.
30. Business Week/ Harris Poll, "How Americans Grade the School System," *Business Week* September 14, 1992, p. 85.
31. Nancy J. Perry, "What We Need to Fix in U.S. Schools," *Fortune,* November 16, 1992, p. 132.
32. "Public's Attitude Toward Public Schools."
33. Wolff, *Where We Stand,* p. 45.
34. Ibid., p. 48.
35. Thurow, *Head to Head,* p. 278.
36. "Public's Attitude Toward Public Schools."
37. Ibid.
38. Segal, "Saving Our Schools."
39. "Public's Attitude Toward Public Schools."
40. Ibid.
41. Ibid.
42. Gideon I. Gartner, "The Crisis in Education," *Management Review,* April 1991.
43. "Public's Attitude Toward Public Schools."
44. Ibid.
45. Reich, *The Next American Frontier,* p. 214.
46. Pearlstein, "Why the Schools Still Don't Work."
47. Wolff, *Where We Stand,* p. 43.
48. "Public's Attitude Toward Public Schools."
49. Ibid.
50. Ibid.

Health Care

1. George Mitchell speech for "Healthamerica Act," May 1991.
2. "CBS News/New York Times Poll," *The New York Times,* August 22, 1991.
3. Mitchell speech for "Healthamerica Act."
4. Ibid.
5. Ibid.
6. Ibid.
7. Ibid.
8. Ibid.

9. "Surgery Needed; Some ABC's of Mediconomics," *The Economist,* July 6, 1991, p. 4.
10. Toby Cohen, "Health Care and the Class Struggle," *The New York Times,* November 17, 1992, Sec. 4, p. 17.
11. Tom Morganthau, "Cutting Through the Gobbledygook," *Newsweek,* February 3, 1992, p. 24.
12. Ronald Henkoff, "Yes, Companies Can Cut Health Costs," *Fortune,* July 1, 1991, p. 53.
13. Mitchell speech for "Healthamerica Act."
14. Henkoff, "Yes, Companies Can Cut Health Costs."
15. Henry J. Aaron, "Looking Backward: 2001–1991—The History of Health Care Financing and Reform Act of 1998," *Brookings Review,* Vol. 9., No. 3 (Summer 1991), pp. 40–45.
16. American Medical Association on "Defensive Medicine" (Washington, D.C.).
17. Ibid.
18. Times Mirror poll, "The People, the Press and Politics on the Eve of 92," December 4, 1991.
19. Gallup poll, August 4, 1991.
20. "CBS News/New York Times Poll," *The New York Times,* August 22, 1991.
21. Ibid.
22. Ibid.
23. Ibid.
24. Ibid.
25. Burton A. Weisbrod, "The Healthcare Quadrilemma: An Essay on Technological Change, Insurance, Quality of Care and Cost Containment," *Journal of Economic Literature,* Vol. XXIX (June 1988), pp. 523–552.
26. Henkoff, "Yes, Companies Can Cut Health Costs."
27. Ibid.
28. Susan Dentzer and Dorian Friedman, "America's Scandalous Health Care," *U.S. News & World Report,* March 12, 1990, p. 24.
29. Steffie Woolhandler, Physicians for a National Health Program.
30. Henkoff, "Yes, Companies Can Cut Health Costs."
31. Lynne M. Tierny, "Poll Shows Americans Want National Health Care Plan and Are Willing to Be Taxed for it," *Nightly Business Report and Reuters,* March 19, 1992.
32. "ABC News/ Washington Post Poll," *The Washington Post,* January 2, 1992.
33. Ibid.
34. Gallup poll, November 3, 1991.
35. Ibid.
36. Tierny, "Poll Shows Americans Want National Health Care Plan."
37. Gallup poll, November 3, 1991.
38. Ibid.
39. Times Mirror poll, "The People, the Press and Politics on the Eve of 92."
40. Gallup poll, May 10, 1991.
41. "Time/CNN Poll," *Time,* December 22, 1991.
42. Health Insurance Association of America, "Health Care," January 14, 1992.

43. "CBS News/New York Times Poll," August 22, 1991.
44. Ibid.
45. Ibid.
46. Henkoff, "Yes, Companies Can Cut Health Costs."
47. Dan Goodgame, "Ready to Operate," *Time,* September 20, 1993, p. 54.

Crime

1. U.S. Department of Justice, Federal Bureau of Investigation, *Uniform Crime Reports 1990* (Washington, D.C.: U.S. Government Printing Office).
2. U.S. Department of Justice, Federal Bureau of Investigation, *Crime in the United States 1990* (Washington, D.C.: U.S. Government Printing Office).
3. Ibid.
4. Ibid.
5. *Uniform Crime Reports 1990,* p. 50.
6. Tom Morganthau, "The War at Home: How to Battle Crime," *Newsweek,* March 25, 1991, p. 35.
7. Ibid.
8. Wolff, *Where We Stand,* p. 289.
9. Ibid., p. 295.
10. *Uniform Crime Reports 1990,* p. 50.
11. *Crime in the United States 1990.*
12. *Uniform Crime Reports 1990,* p. 50.
13. Ibid., p. 174.
14. Ibid., p. 50.
15. *Crime in the United States 1990.*
16. *Uniform Crime Reports 1990,* p. 50.
17. Ibid., p. 174.
18. Ibid., pp. 191, 199.
19. Ibid., p. 21.
20. Ibid., p. 21.
21. Ibid., p. 50.
22. *Crime in the United States 1990.*
23. *Uniform Crime Reports 1990,* p. 50.
24. Ibid., p. 174.
25. Ibid., p. 16.
26. Ibid., p. 50.
27. *Crime in the United States 1990.*
28. *Uniform Crime Reports 1990,* p. 50.
29. Ibid., p. 174.
30. Ibid., p. 14.
31. Ibid., pp. 11–13.
32. Ibid.
33. Morganthau, "The War at Home."
34. *Uniform Crime Reports 1990,* p. 13.
35. Ibid., p. 12.

36. *Gallup Poll Monthly,* Report No. 318 (Princeton, N.J.: Gallup Poll, March 1992), pp. 51, 52.
37. Ibid.
38. Ibid.
39. National Victim Center, "America Speaks Out: Citizens' Attitudes About Victims' Rights and Violence" (Fort Worth, Texas: National Victim Center, April 1991).
40. U.S. Department of Justice, *Drugs and Jail Inmates* (August 1991).
41. Ibid.
42. Ibid.
43. U.S. Department of Justice, *Profile of Jail Inmates, 1989* (April 1991).
44. *Crime in the United States 1990.*
45. Gordon Witkin, Ted Gest, and Dorian Friedman, "Cops Under Fire," *U.S. News & World Report,* December 3, 1990, p. 32.
46. Jerald G. Bachman, Lloyd D. Johnston, and Patrick O'Malley, *Monitoring the Future* (Ann Arbor, Mich.: Institute for Social Research, University of Michigan).
47. Witkin, Gest, and Friedman, "Cops Under Fire."
48. Ibid.
49. Tristram Coffin, "Crime in the Cities," *Washington Spectator,* June 1, 1991.
50. National Victim Center, "America Speaks Out."
51. *Crime in the United States 1990.*
52. Ibid.
53. Witkin, Gest, and Friedman, "Cops Under Fire."
54. Ibid.
55. Richard J. Ludman, *Police Behavior: A Sociological Perspective* (New York: Oxford University Press, 1980).
56. *Gallup Poll Monthly,* Report No. 318.
57. *Crime in the United States 1990.*
58. Briam Dumaine, "New Weapons in the Crime War," *Fortune,* June 3, 1991, p. 180.
59. U.S. Department of Justice, *Correctional Populations in the United States 1990* (July, 1992).
60. Ibid.
61. Dumaine, "New Weapons in the Crime War."
62. Morganthau, "The War at Home."
63. Dumaine, "New Weapons in the Crime War."
64. *Gallup Poll Monthly,* Report No. 318.
65. U.S. Department of Justice, *Correctional Populations in the United States 1990.*
66. James Allan Davis and Tom W. Smith, *General Social Surveys 1972–1992* (Chicago: National Opinion Research Center, University of Chicago).
67. Dumaine, "New Weapons in the Crime War."
68. Coffin, "Crime in the Cities."
69. *Uniform Crime Reports 1990,* p. 50.
70. *Gallup Poll Monthly,* Report No. 318.
71. Ibid.
72. Davis and Smith, General Social Surveys 1972–1992.
73. *Gallup Poll Monthly,* Report No. 318.

Drugs

1. Mark S. Gold, M.D., "Successful Strategies for Combatting Casual Drug Use: Successful Treatment Programs for Cocaine and Crack," *The Heritage Lectures,* No. 297 (March 20–21, 1990), p. 26.

2. Carlton E. Turner, "Status of Drug Use in America: Recent Trends in American Drug Use," *The Heritage Lectures,* No. 297 (March 20–21, 1990), p. 7.

3. Joel W. Hay, "The Harm They Do to Others: A Primer on the External Costs of Drug Abuse," *Searching for Alternatives: Drug Control Policy in the United States,* ed. Melvyn B. Krauss and Edward Lazear (Stanford, Calif.: Hoover Institution Press, 1991) p. 206.

4. U.S. Department of Justice, National Institute of Justice, *1990 Drug Use Forecasting Annual Reports,* August 1991, pp. 5, 7–9.

5. James K. Stewart, "Hard Core Drug Abuse and Its Consequences: The Connection Between Drug Use and Urban Crime," *The Heritage Lectures,* No. 297 (March 20–21, 1990), p. 57.

6. U.S. Department of Justice, National Institute of Justice, *Research in Action,* March–April 1988, p. 208.

7. Stewart, "Hard Core Drug Abuse and Its Consequences."

8. U.S. Department of Justice, National Institute of Justice, *Research in Action.*

9. Katherine Snow, "Drug Tests Getting High Grades," *The Business Journal of Charlotte Inc.,* November 9, 1992.

10. Turner, "Status of Drug Use in America."

11. Ibid.

12. Ibid.

13. Lloyd D. Johnston, Patrick M. O'Malley, and Gerald G. Bachman, *Smoking, Drinking and Illicit Drug Use Among American Secondary School Students, College Students and Young Adults 1975–1991* (Washington, D.C.: U.S. Department of Health and Human Services, National Institute on Drug Abuse, 1992).

14. Mathea Falco, *The Making of a Drug Free America: Programs That Work* (New York: Times Books, 1992), pp.8–9.

15. Daniel Klaidman, "How Tough on Crime? The President-Elect Has Avoided the Soft-on-Crime Label, but He's Likely to Change the Terms of the Drug War to Emphasize Treatment," *The Recorder,* November 9, 1992, p. 1.

16. James Ostrowski, "Thinking About Drug Legalization," *The Crisis in Drug Prohibition,* ed. David Boaz (Washington, D.C.: Cato Institute, 1990), p. 59.

17. Robert E. Peterson, "Legalization: The Myth Exposed," *Searching for Alternatives: Drug Control Policy in the United States,* ed. Melvyn B. Krauss and Edward Lazear (Stanford, Calif.: Hoover Institution Press, 1991), p. 328.

18. Ibid., p. 342.

19. Ibid., p. 332.

20. Ibid., p. 333.

21. Ibid., p. 343.

22. Ibid., p. 335.

23. Ibid., p. 342.

24. Falco, *The Making of a Drug Free America,* pp. 8–9.
25. Ibid.
26. Ibid., pp. 223–224.
27. Gordon Witkin and Ted Gest, "Street Crime: An Agenda for Change," *U.S. News & World Report,* October 5, 1992, p. 126.
28. Joseph B. Treaster, "Echoes of Prohibition: 20 Years of War on Drugs and No Victory Yet," *The New York Times,* June 14, 1992, Sec. 4, p. 7.
29. Falco, *The Making of a Drug Free America,* pp. 134–135.
30. Ibid.
31. Ibid., pp. 138–141.
32. Rick Nash, "Stopping Drug Use in Schools: The DARE Program," *The Heritage Lectures,* No. 297 (March 20–21, 1990), p. 52.
33. Falco, *The Making of a Drug Free America,* p.165.
34. Turner, "Status of Drug Use in America."

PART III

The Deficit

1. Carol Cox Wait, *The Best Things in Life Are Not Free,* (Washington, D.C.: Committee for a Responsible Federal Budget, 1993).
2. Ibid.

AIDS

1. U.S. Department of Health and Human Services, Vital Health Statistics of the Centers for Disease and Prevention, *AIDS Knowledge and Attitudes for 1991: Data from the National Health Interview Survey* (Washington, D.C., 1991).
2. Quotes from the Centers for Disease Control (Washington, D.C.).
3. Ibid.
4. Ibid.
5. Ibid.
6. AIDS Action Council, "AIDS in the U.S. as of September 31, 1991" (Washington, D.C.).
7. Quotes from the Centers for Disease Control.
8. AIDS Action Council, "AIDS in the U.S."
9. U.S. Department of Health and Human Services, *AIDS Knowledge and Attitudes.*
10. Fred D. Hellinger, "The National Forecasts of the Medical Care Costs of AIDS: 1988–1992," *Inquire 25,* Winter 1988, pp. 469–484.
11. AIDS Action Council, "AIDS in the U.S."
12. Robert F. Black, Sara Collins, and Don L. Boroughs, "The Hidden Cost of AIDS," *U.S. News & World Report,* July 27, 1992.

Poverty

1. Bureau of the Census, Economics and Statistics Administration, *Poverty in the United States* (Washington, D.C., 1991), p. 16.
2. Ibid.

3. Ibid.
4. Ibid.
5. R. H. Ropers, *Persistent Poverty: The American Dream Turned Nightmare* (New York: Plenum, 1991).
6. Bureau of the Census, *Poverty in the United States.*
7. Ropers, *Persistent Poverty.*
8. Bureau of the Census, *Poverty in the United States.*
9. Ropers, *Persistent Poverty.*
10. Ibid.
11. Ibid.
12. Ibid.
13. Gordon Berliner and William McAllister, "Homeless: Why Nothing Has Worked and What Will," *Brookings Review,* Fall 1992, p. 12.

Homelessness

1. Peter Rossi, *Down and Out in America: The Origins of Homelessness* (Chicago: University of Chicago Press, 1991).
2. Berliner and McAllister, "Homeless."
3. U.S. Department of Housing and Urban Development, "Homelessness" (Rockville, Md: HUD).
4. "Rougher and Tougher," *The Economist,* June 29, 1991, p. 21.
5. E. Fuller Torrey, "Who Goes Homeless," *The National Review,* August 26, 1991, p. 34.
6. Ibid.

The Environment

1. J. Walter Thompson U.S.A., *JWT Greenwatch,* Vol. 1, No. 2 (1992).
2. Ibid.
3. Ibid.
4. Ibid.

PART IV

Racism

1. Marc Whitaker, "A Crisis of Shattered Dreams," *Newsweek,* May 6, 1991, p. 28.
2. Ibid.
3. Studs Terkel, *Race: How Blacks and Whites Think About the American Obsession* (New York: New Press, 1992).
4. Thomas Byrne Edsall, "Race," *The Atlantic,* May 1991, p. 56.
5. Andrew Billingsley, "Understanding African American Family Diversity," in National Urban League, *The State of Black America 1990* (New York: National Urban League, 1990).
6. Davidson and Rees-Mogg, *The Great Reckoning,* p. 294.
7. Edsall, "Race."
8. Whitaker, "A Crisis of Shattered Dreams."

9. Ibid.
10. Edsall, "Race."

Gun Control

1. Davis and Smith, *General Social Surveys 1972–1992.*
2. Handgun Control Inc., Washington, D.C.
3. Ibid.
4. Coalition to Stop Gun Violence, "FBI Statistics" (Washington, D.C.).
5. Ibid.
6. Michael K. Beard, "Still Time to Cancel Your Order," *Los Angeles Times, Washington edition,* May 19, 1992, p. A11.
7. Coalition to Stop Gun Violence, "FBI Statistics."
8. Handgun Control Inc.
9. Ibid.
10. Coalition to Stop Gun Violence, "Handgun Fact Sheet."
11. Ibid.
12. Ibid.
13. NRA, Institute for Legislative Action, *NRA Firearms Fact Sheet* (Washington, D.C.: NRA, December 1992).
14. NRA, Institute for Legislative Action, *Ten Myths About Gun Control* (Washington, D.C.: NRA, December 1992).
15. NRA, Institute for Legislative Action, *NRA Firearms Fact Sheet.*
16. James Wright and Peter Rossi, *The Armed Criminal in America* (Washington, D.C.: U.S. Department of Justice).
17. NRA, Institute for Legislative Action, *NRA Firearms Fact Sheet.*
18. Ibid.
19. Joshua Horwitz, "The Second Amendment Allows Militias to Have Guns—Not You," *The Philadelphia Inquirer* December 20, 1991, p. 19A.
20. Ibid.
21. NRA, Institute for Legislative Action, *NRA Firearms Fact Sheet.*

Abortion

1. The Alan Guttmacher Institute, "Facts in Brief: Abortion in the United States" (Washington, D.C., January 4, 1993).
2. Ibid.
3. Ibid.
4. Wolff, *Where We Stand,* p. 264.
5. The Alan Guttmacher Institute, "Facts in Brief: Abortion in the United States."
6. Wolff, *Where We Stand,* pp. 250–251.
7. The Alan Guttmacher Institute, "Facts in Brief: Abortion in the United States."
8. Ibid.
9. Ibid.
10. "How to End the Abortion War," *The New York Times,* January 1992, p. 26.
11. The National Abortion Federation.

12. Linda Racovich, "Before Roe v. Wade; Desperation; After Roe Is Reversed," *The Progressive,* January 1992, p. 18.

Sexual Discrimination and Harassment

1. The Women's Legal Defense Fund, "Sexual Harassment in the Workplace" (Washington, D.C.).
2. Ibid.
3. Ibid.
4. Ibid.
5. Ibid.
6. Equal Employment Opportunity Commission, Washington, D.C.
7. The Women's Legal Defense Fund, "Sexual Harassment in the Workplace."
8. Ibid.
9. Ibid.